THEODORE OF MOPSUESTIA AND MODERN THOUGHT

THEODORE OF MOPSUESTIA AND MODERN THOUGHT

BY
L. PATTERSON, B.D.

WIPF & STOCK · Eugene, Oregon

Wipf and Stock Publishers
199 W 8th Ave, Suite 3
Eugene, OR 97401

Theodore of Mopsuestia and Modern Thought
By Patterson, L., B. D.
ISBN 13: 978-1-61097-235-2
Publication date 2/3/2011
Previously published by SPCK, 1926

INTRODUCTION

ARCHBISHOP TEMPLE, writing to his friend Dr. Scott in 1857, made this striking statement : " Our theology has been cast in a scholastic mode, *i.e.* all based on Logic. We are in need of, and we are being gradually forced into a theology based on psychology." This antithesis appears to be more epigrammatic than exact. It would hardly be too much to say that there has been no period of Church history when theology has not been closely connected with psychology. The great scholastic theologians were strongly influenced by psychology, especially that of Aristotle. The main difference between the scholastic psychology and modern theories is that the Schoolmen laid special emphasis on the conscious activities of reason and will, while the new psychologists direct their attention to the subconscious elements of the mind, such as the instincts and complexes.

Even then, the Schoolmen did not, in that respect, initiate a new movement in theology. The Church fathers of the first four or five centuries were influenced by the psychology of Plato and Aristotle. This was a natural and necessary development of Christian theology. When the fathers attempted to elaborate the truths of the

INTRODUCTION

Gospel into a dogmatic system, they were obliged to express their ideas in the terms of contemporary philosophy. Besides, theology ought to be combined with psychology, when the two sciences come in contact, as in the doctrines of man, sin, and the Incarnation.

It is our present purpose to examine the theology of Theodore of Mopsuestia, who is the best representative of the school of Antioch, and to discover what value it can have for us at the present time. The school of Antioch has been relatively neglected, owing to the greater prominence of the leaders of the school of Alexandria. Yet it is almost a truism to say that " the two standpoints, the Alexandrian and the Antiochene, represent complementary aspects of Christian theology." Speaking generally, the Alexandrian method was deductive, and its philosophical basis was Platonic: the Antiochene method was inductive, and based on the philosophy of Aristotle. The Alexandrian interpretation of Scripture was allegorical and mystical, while the Antiochene was literal and historical.

Again, they differed in their psychology. The Alexandrians inclined to the threefold division of man into body, soul, and spirit, and so may be called trichotomists. The Antiochenes preferred the twofold division into body and soul, and were, therefore, dichotomists. The former view was, probably but not certainly, held by the later writers of the Old Testament: it was the dominant view of St. Paul, but it is doubtful whether it can be derived from the teaching of Plato or the Stoics. The latter view was based on the earlier doctrine of the Old Testament and that of the Gospels, and was supported by the general teaching of Aristotle.

Lastly, the writer finds himself in substantial agreement with the statement of a Roman Catholic theologian, Père J. Mahé, that "the two Christologies of Antioch and Alexandria, in spite of notable differences, were, in the main, both perfectly orthodox." It is true that the former laid predominant emphasis on the manhood, and the latter on the Godhead of our Lord. The writer does not wish to disguise his preference for the school of Antioch, which, in his opinion, agrees best with modern science and psychology : but he realizes that both schools were needed to preserve the balance of truth. There were heretics in both schools, just as there may be black sheep in every fold. If Antioch is to be condemned for the errors of Paul of Samosata and Nestorius, Alexandria was responsible for the Arian and Apollinarian heresies. It would be fair to say that, while both schools employed their distinctive methods, each of them endeavoured to maintain and to expound the perfect union of God and man in the Incarnation.

CONTENTS

INTRODUCTION v

CHAPTER I
THEODORE'S LIFE AND WORKS . . . 1

CHAPTER II
DOCTRINE OF MAN 13

CHAPTER III
DOCTRINE OF GOD AND CHRIST . . . 23

CHAPTER IV
SALVATION, THE CHURCH, AND THE SACRAMENTS 47

CHAPTER V
THE LAST THINGS AND THE FUTURE LIFE . 58

CHAPTER VI

THEODORE'S RELATION TO MODERN THOUGHT . . . 67

CHAPTER VII

THE RESULTANT DOCTRINE 94

INDEX 113

THEODORE OF MOPSUESTIA AND MODERN THOUGHT

CHAPTER I

HIS LIFE AND WORKS [1]

THEODORE, generally known by the surname "of Mopsuestia," was born at Antioch about A.D. 350. His father was, apparently, a man of some wealth and held an official position at Antioch.[2] His brother, Polychronius, became Bishop of Apamea on the Orontes ; his cousin, Pæanius, held important posts, and was probably promoted to some high office at Constantinople.[3] However, none of them

---

[1] The chief modern authorities for the life and teaching of Theodore are O. F. Fritzsche, *de Theod. M. vita et scriptis* (1836) ; H. Kihn, *Theodor u. Junilius* (1880) ; H. B. Swete, Edition of the *Commentaries on the Epistles of St. Paul* (vol. i. 1880, vol. ii. 1882), and his article in the *Dictionary of Christian Biography,* vol. iv (1887). A general description of the Antiochene theology is given by J. H. Srawley in the *Encyclopædia of Religion and Ethics*, vol. i, pp. 584–93 (1908). Short sketches of Theodore are found in J. F. Bethune-Baker, *Introduction to the Early History of Christian Doctrine*, pp. 256–60 (1903), Bardenhewer, *Geschichte der altchristlichen Literatur*, and B. J. Kidd, *History of the Church*, vol. iii, pp. 196–201 (1922).

[2] Chrysostom, *ad Theod. lapsum*, ii.

[3] Ib. *Epp.* 95, 193, 204, 220. The last seems to refer to Pæanius's promotion.

2 THEODORE OF MOPSUESTIA

exercised so much authority and influence over the youthful Theodore as his friend and companion, John Chrysostom. They attended together the lectures of the sophist Libanius,[1] and possibly other philosophers; they both retired from the world to the monastic school of Diodore of Tarsus.[2] Chrysostom declares that Theodore's conversion was sincere and fervent,[3] and suggests by his words that Theodore was baptized about this time.[4] Theodore devoted himself to reading of the Scriptures and to prayer, and practised zealously and cheerfully every form of self-discipline. But his new-born enthusiasm was followed by a sudden reaction. Theodore was fascinated by the charms of a beautiful girl named Hermione,[5] and thought of marrying her and returning to the secular life.[6] He was persuaded by the earnest appeal of Chrysostom to abandon this project and remain true to his monastic vows. Still, this early disappointment (for he was not yet twenty years old),[7] and the blighting of his youthful love, may have cast a gloom over his later life.

From 369 to 378 Theodore remained under the spiritual direction of Diodore, who was then elevated to the see of Tarsus. Theodore attached himself subsequently to Flavian, Bishop of Antioch, and was ordained priest by him in 383, three years before

---

[1] Socr. *Eccl. Hist.* vi. 3. [2] Theodoret, *H.E.* v. 39.

[3] *ad Th. laps.* ii. 1.

[4] *Ib.* i. 1. The temple (of Th.'s soul): τῇ τοῦ πνεύματος ἀπέστιλβε χάριτι.

[5] *Ib.* 13. [6] Soz. *H.E.* viii. 2. [7] *ad. Th. laps.* ii. 4.

HIS LIFE AND WORKS 3

Chrysostom's ordination to the priesthood. His friend's greater powers as a preacher, or the visit of his old master Diodore to Antioch, may have induced Theodore to remove to Tarsus. He stayed there till 392, when he was consecrated to the see of Mopsuestia [1] in the province of Cilicia.

His episcopate, which lasted for thirty-six years (392–428),[2] was fairly peaceful, and was not conspicuous either by success or failure. He accompanied Flavian to a synod held at Constantinople in 394, and preached a sermon there which made a deep impression on the Emperor Theodosius I.[3] On the whole, Theodore was spared the bitterness of political intrigue and ecclesiastical controversy, from which Chrysostom suffered. One of the most admirable features of Theodore's character was his constant affection for Chrysostom, which was not altered either by prosperity or adversity. Chrysostom pays a glowing tribute to Theodore's loyal friendship. He says that he " can never forget the love of Theodore, so genuine and warm, so sincere and guileless, a love maintained from early years, and manifested even now."[4] Chrysostom thanks Theodore for the efforts that he has made for his release from exile. " I am not unaware of all that you have endeavoured to say and do on my behalf."[5]

---

[1] The name of the town is interpreted as the dwelling of Mopsus, the legendary King of the Argives (Strabo, *Geographica*, xiv. 5).

[2] Theodoret, *H.E.* v. 39.

[3] *Sic* John of Antioch (in Facundus, *pro Defens. Tr. Capitul.* ii. 2).

[4] Chrys. *Ep.* 112.   [5] *Ib.* cp. *Ep.* 204 (to Pæanius).

Theodore did not bear the brunt of theological controversies which rose to their height after his death. The storm which was brewing over the title Θεοτόκος had not yet burst. Theodore is reported to have given offence by a sermon which he preached on this subject,[1] but he retracted these statements and expressed himself in other writings with studious moderation and strict impartiality.

Again, when Julian of Eclanum and the other Pelagian leaders were driven from the West in 418, they found a refuge with Theodore till 422. During these years Theodore probably wrote his treatise on Original Sin, which did not apparently attract much notice at the time.[2]

Towards the end of the year 428, Theodore died, worn out by fifty years of literary and pastoral work.[3] Though he had taken his share in doctrinal controversy, he departed in the peace of the Church and with an unsullied reputation. There could be no better epitaph inscribed upon his grave than the words, " Felix non vitæ tantum claritate, sed etiam opportunitate mortis ! "[4]

His orthodoxy was never seriously impugned till after his death. Cyril of Alexandria asserts that the Eastern bishops begged him not to condemn Theodore's writings, on the ground that the people

---

[1] John of Antioch, *ap.* Fac. *op. cit.* x. 2.
[2] Its date is given as not earlier than 419 by Swete, vol. i. lx, note.
[3] Theodt. *H.E.* v. 39, Fac. ii. 2.
[4] Quoted by Dr. Swete from Tacitus, *Agricola*, chap. 45.

HIS LIFE AND WORKS 5

used to exclaim in the churches, "We believe as Theodore believed; long live the faith of Theodore."[1] But while he was strongly supported by John of Antioch, Ibas of Edessa, and Theodoret of Cyrrhus, he was vigorously opposed by Marius Mercator, Cyril of Alexandria, and finally by Leontius of Byzantium. About 431 Marius Mercator denounced Theodore both as the author of the Pelagian heresy and as the forerunner of Nestorianism. Rabbulas, Bishop of Edessa till 435, supported Theodore and the rest of his school at the Council of Ephesus, but afterwards turned against him. Cyril was encouraged by Rabbulas's example and exhortation to attack Theodore with whole-hearted vigour.[2] But to do him justice, Cyril was restrained by feelings of Christian charity and human decency from defaming the character of the dead.[3] He urged that it would be sufficient to condemn the opinions of Theodore without anathematizing him, as he had gone to his rest.[4] That was, at least, a slight concession to Christian sentiment.

However, the final blow at Theodore's reputation was dealt by the Council of Constantinople in 553. The Three Chapters (*i.e.* the writings of Theodore,

[1] Cyril, *Ep.* 69.
[2] Ib. *Epp.* 67, 71, 72.
[3] We fear that Theodoret was not so scrupulous with regard to Cyril (*Ep.* 180, " Sero tandem et vix malus homo defunctus est "). Dr. Kidd, however, rejects this letter as not genuine (*op. cit.* vol. iii. 261, 263). The maxim, " De mortuis nil nisi bonum," was seldom observed by ancient theologians.
[4] Cyril, *Ep.* 72.

6 THEODORE OF MOPSUESTIA

Ibas, and Theodoret) had been previously criticized by the Emperor Justinian, acting on the advice of certain bishops, in the Edict of 545, and in the second Edict, or Confession of Faith, in 551.[1] But the political intrigues and theological motives which prompted the condemnation of Theodore might well make us pause before accepting the decision of the Council of Constantinople. The Emperor was determined to secure the unity of the Church at any price, and had been strongly influenced by his Empress Theodora, and her Monophysite coterie.[2] It is certainly difficult to justify or approve on these grounds the anathema pronounced against Theodore at the Council of 553.

Theodore's literary work, with which we are chiefly concerned, was partly exegetical and partly doctrinal. His followers called him "the interpreter," and he was certainly the most remarkable and original representative of the Antiochene school of Biblical interpretation. Even if we make allowance for the exaggeration of his admirers,[3] and for the fact that much less of his work has been preserved, it is probable that his commentaries on Scripture were almost as numerous as those of his fellow-student Chrysostom. He began his exegetical work with a commentary on the Psalter. We may

[1] The Judicatum of 548, which condemned the Three Chapters, was soon recalled. Strictly speaking, the Three Chapters or Articles contained the teaching of Theodore and the others, which was condemned by Justinian.

[2] It is true that Theodora died in 548, but her influence over Justinian was paramount up to that year.

[3] Facundus, ii. 2, x. 4.

HIS LIFE AND WORKS 7

discount the sarcastic remark of Leontius [1] that Theodore was playing tricks with Holy Scripture when he was not more than eighteen years old (A.D. 368), as it is more probable that the work was composed towards the end of the period during which Theodore was attending the lectures of Diodore (*i.e.* before 378). He admitted himself that the work was carelessly written, but pleaded his youthful inexperience and unsettled circumstances.[2] It is true that he anticipated in some of his comments the extreme hypotheses of modern criticism, but, in the main, his conclusions have been verified by sound and sober scholarship.[3] He accepted only four Psalms (Nos. 2, 8, 45, and 110) as directly referring to the Messiah, but he was prepared to admit that other Psalms, such as the 16th and the 22nd, might be applied to Christ in a secondary sense.[4] In his exegesis of the rest of the Old Testament, Theodore reveals most clearly the merits and defects of Antiochene hermeneutics. Like Diodore [5]

---

[1] τοῦτόν φασιν ὀκτω πρὸς τοῖς δέκα καὶ οὐ πλείονας ἄγοντα χρόνους κατὰ τῶν ἱερῶν παροινῆσαι γραφῶν (Migne, *P.G.* lxxxvi. 1364).

[2] Fac. *op. cit.* iii. 6. Dr. Swete argues in favour of the later date (*Epistles of St. Paul*, vol. i, lx, note).

[3] *E.g.* it is generally admitted that the headings of the Psalms are not to be accepted without question, and that many Psalms are Exilic or Maccabæan (*cp.* Hastings, *D.B.* p. 772 [1910]).

[4] *E.g.* the 22nd Psalm is a narrative of David's conflict with Absalom; yet it is rightly taken by the Evangelist to describe the Passion of Christ.

[5] Diodore, commenting on Gen. xlix. 11, said, "We think it right for them to know, that we infinitely prefer the historical interpretation to the allegorical" (Migne, *P.G.* xxxiii. 1580).

8 THEODORE OF MOPSUESTIA

and Chrysostom,[1] Theodore concentrated his attention on the historical meaning of Scripture. Photius said of Theodore's commentary on Genesis, that " he avoided the allegorical method which was possible for him, and gave an historical interpretation."[2] On the other hand, he believed that the typical or symbolic sense of Scripture, if it was based on the literal sense, was also intended by God.[3] Generally speaking, he does not deny that the historical events and the prophecies of the Old Testament are a preparation for the Gospel, in which is found their complete fulfilment.

Turning to the New Testament, we may pass over the Gospels and the Acts, as they are only preserved in a few fragments. The Pauline Epistles, of which the greater part survives only in a Latin translation of the original text, afford the clearest conspectus of Theodore's teaching. In particular, we may refer to the commentary on the Epistle to the Galatians as bearing on Theodore's view of the right and wrong use of allegory.[4] He makes a

[1] Chrysostom, contrasting his interpretation of Paradise with that of Origen, said, " My advice is that we should close our ears to all such arguments and follow to the end the rule of Holy Scripture."

[2] Photius, *bibl. Cod.* 38.

[3] Theodore's introduction to Jonah states that ancient history was found to be a type of later events (τύπος τις τὰ παλαιὰ τῶν ὑστέρων).

[4] Gal. iv. 24 (Swete, vol. i, pp. 73–83). *Cp.* Theodore's work in 5 volumes, *Against the Allegorizers*, mentioned by Facundus (iii. 6). [For convenience, we shall quote the chapter and verse of the particular Epistle, not the volume or page in Dr. Swete's commentary.]

HIS LIFE AND WORKS 9

vigorous onslaught on those commentators who turn the meaning of Holy Scripture upside down, and invent foolish fables, to which they give the name of allegory. The Apostle, he says, does not destroy history, but uses it for his own understanding of the facts. No doubt Theodore is attacking Origen, but the instance which he takes is rather unfortunate. He sneers at the " spiritual " interpretation of Genesis as making out that Adam is not Adam, Paradise not Paradise, the snake not a snake.[1] If that were true, then St. Paul's saying about the serpent beguiling Eve would be out of place and meaningless. On the contrary, we should agree with Origen that the story cannot be accepted as literal history, and we should not concede to Theodore that the allegorical view does away with the facts of sin and salvation through Christ.

St. Paul, according to Theodore, means by allegory the comparison, by juxtaposition, of past with present events.[2] This definition fits better the treatment of the story of Abraham and Sarah. Theodore follows St. Paul in his interpretation of Sarah and Hagar as the two covenants, or the earthly and the heavenly Jerusalem, but he diverges from him in his own exposition of " Jerusalem which is above." By these words, he says, the Apostle is not making up dreams, like those who think that everything should be thrown into an allegorical form, but by the second covenant he

[1] *Cp*. Origen, in *Gen*. ii. 9, *de princ*. iv. 16.
[2] Swete, vol. i, p. 79. As Theodore says elsewhere, ancient history is a *type* of future events.

means the resurrection or heavenly life, which we shall enjoy with Christ. This is hardly a possible explanation of St. Paul's phrase, which, at the most, can only refer to the Church expectant in heaven as well as militant on earth.

Again, Theodore agrees with St. Paul's exposition of the history of the wanderings and temptations of the Israelites in the wilderness as a type of Christian life and experience. It is evident that he understood St. Paul to use allegory in that sense, and modern scholars are inclined to think that he was right.[1] We may, perhaps, be more qualified to estimate the merits and demerits of allegory than ancient theologians. Allegory may deliver us from the tyranny of verbal inspiration, but it ought not to plunge us into the anarchy of fantastic imagination. The literal or historical sense of any passage of Scripture should be considered in the first place: but no one would be so narrow and short-sighted as to deny the deeper and more spiritual meaning of many passages in the Old and New Testament.

Last of all, the surviving fragments of Theodore's dogmatic treatises must be mentioned. He is reported to have written fifteen books on the Incarnation, while he was still a priest at Antioch (383-392).[2] Besides this work, a second treatise

---

[1] *Cp*. Dr. Lightfoot in his commentary on the Epistle to the Galatians (1902), p. 199. " With St. Paul, Hagar's career is an allegory, because it is a history. The symbol and the thing symbolized are the same in kind."

[2] Fac. ix. 3, and Gennadius (*de Viris illustr.* 12).

HIS LIFE AND WORKS

" on Apollinarius " is ascribed to him by Facundus, who quotes Theodore's statement that he wrote this thirty years later than the former (*i.e.* about 413). Thirdly, there is the treatise on Original Sin, which was written about 419. The title of the work is given by Marius Mercator as " against St. Augustine defending original sin," but it is more correctly quoted by Photius as " against those who assert that men sin by nature and not by deliberate purpose (γνώμη)."[1] Lastly, Theodore delivered some catechetical lectures, to which was probably appended an Ecthesis, or Exposition of the Faith. This document was produced at the Council of Ephesus in 431 by Charisius, presbyter of Philadelphia, and condemned without mention of the author's name.[2]

Little or nothing remains of Theodore's lesser dogmatic treatises; but his three books on " Persian Magic " would have been a valuable contribution to the study of comparative religion if they had been preserved. Zoroastrianism, in its later forms, exercised a certain influence upon the Western world, while the cognate system of Manichæism had proved a serious rival to Christianity. On the other hand, Christian missionaries, under the auspices of Nestorius and his followers, penetrated to Persia and the further East.[3] This movement, no doubt,

[1] Photius, *bibl. Cod.* 177.
[2] Facundus (iii. 2) denies that Theodore is the author, in spite of its similarity to the rest of his teaching, but Mercator attributes it to him, and attacks him on these grounds.
[3] Cosmas Indicopleustes vouches for their influence, about A.D. 547, in India.

owed its early inspiration to Theodore, and this is a sufficient proof that the church of Antioch was, at all stages of its history, imbued with the spirit of evangelistic enthusiasm.

However, we depend chiefly upon Theodore's commentary on the Pauline Epistles and his dogmatic treatises for our reconstruction of his doctrinal system. His teaching may be conveniently considered under four main heads, (*a*) anthropology, (*b*) Christology, (*c*) soteriology, (*d*) eschatology. It is inevitable that these sections will occasionally overlap one another, but this division will make for clearness and avoid unnecessary confusion.

CHAPTER II

THE DOCTRINE OF MAN

THEODORE'S conception of man bears a twofold relation both to the universe and to God. The universe is, so to speak, one body, composed of many members, intelligible beings as well as sensible phenomena. God made one living creature, that is, man, consisting of a visible body and an invisible soul.[1] The body is compounded of four elements, earth, air, fire, and water, like the material creation. By his body man is linked with the visible natures; he claims kinship with the invisible natures by his soul. Man is, as it were, the friendly bond [2] of the whole creation, because all things are united in him. In consequence, all elements of the universe are connected with man by a sympathetic affinity, and operate for his benefit. Sensible phenomena move because of man's need, while the intelligible powers preside over phenomena, moving them for man's advantage and ministering to his salvation.[3]

[1] Rom. viii. 19, Eph. i. 10, and *de Apollin*. bk. iv, fr. 1. Theodore is a convinced dichotomist, like Diodore (*Comm. in Ps.* 71^{23}) and Chrysostom, *Hom.* vii. *in Phil.* chap. 3. This view was essential to Theodore's theology.

[2] φιλίας ἐνέχυρον, and σύνδεσμος.

[3] Theodore quotes Heb. i. 14. He accepts the Pauline authorship of this Epistle.

But man possesses an even higher affinity than that which he claims with created beings ·in the spiritual world. Man was made in the image and likeness of God. The testimony of Genesis is confirmed by the words of St. Paul, designating man as the image and glory of God.[1] He is the visible representative of God, and is entitled to receive the homage of all creation.[2]

However, man has not yet fulfilled this noble purpose or attained this sublime destiny. He is still far removed from what he ought to be. Corresponding to man's physical and spiritual condition, there are two states of life.[3] The first state is mutable, and exposed to temptation and mortality; the second is immutable, and entirely free from sin and death.[4] Adam was the beginner of the former mortal state, while the second immortal state was initiated by Christ.[5]

The original state of man, then, was mortality.[6] Similar views were stated or suggested by earlier teachers of the church of Antioch. Theophilus asserted that "God made man neither immortal

---

[1] Theodore quotes Gen. i. 27 and 1 Cor. xi. 7 in his exposition of Col. i. 15 as referring to the manhood of our Lord.

[2] Cp. *de Incarn.* bk. xii. fr. 5, where Heb. i. 6 is taken as referring to our Lord as man.

[3] καταστάσεις. The word means a condition of body or of soul (Plato, *Rep.* 547B).

[4] *Comm. in Gen.* (Migne, lxvi. 654).

[5] Rom. vii. 4. *On Orig. Sin*, bk. iii, fr. 3, Ecthesis (Swete, *op. cit.* vol. ii, p. 331).

[6] Man's formation from the earth was the condition and sign of his mortality (*Orig. Sin*, bk. iv).

THE DOCTRINE OF MAN 15

nor yet mortal, but capable of both states."[1] Again, Chrysostom affirmed that "God made not the soul mortal, but permitted it to be immortal."[2] No doubt Theodore could have combined the two views by stating that man has an immortal soul and a mortal body:[3] but he was specially anxious to maintain that man was not wholly immortal at the first moment of his creation.

The Fall did not make any change in God's original purpose or man's natural condition. Theodore describes as utter madness the belief that either God made man immortal and then changed His mind, or He did not know that Adam would sin. It is absurd to suppose that God made man immortal for six hours, and then showed him to be mortal after sin. It is certain, that if God had wished him to be immortal, not even the intervention of sin would have changed His purpose. God knew that Adam would sin, and on that account would doubtless die.[4]

Again, God did not say, "Ye shall be mortal, but ye shall surely die." Death was the sentence pronounced upon our first parents for their sin, but its execution was deferred according to God's lovingkindness.[5]

Theodore seems to admit that Adam's sin affected

---

[1] Theophilus, *ad Autolycum*, bk. ii. xxvii.
[2] Chrysostom, *Hom. on the Statues*, xi. 3.
[3] *Cp.* Theodoret, *Ep.* 145. "Every man has an immortal soul, and a mortal body."
[4] *Orig. Sin*, bk. iii, fr. 1. *Cp.* Gal. ii. 15.
[5] *Orig. Sin*, bk. iv. If the literal interpretation were pressed, Adam survived for 930 years (Gen. v. 5).

not only himself, but his posterity.[1] Adam's sin made the rest of men mortal, and on that account prone to sin.[2] But, even then, they suffered for their own sins, and were not punished on account of Adam's transgression.[3] It would surely be unjust that righteous Abel should suffer the penalty of sin, which is death, while his guilty parents outlived him. Again, it is highly incongruous to suppose that Noah, Abraham, Moses, and David were punished for the solitary offence of Adam. Lastly, Enoch was not preserved from death, because he was so much more pious than other men. On the contrary, God translated him, because He had decreed from the beginning that men should be mortal at first, but afterwards enjoy immortality.[4]

The doctrine of men being punished for Adam's sin is destructive of moral responsibility. Men received the sentence of death as a penalty for their own sins, though these were different in kind from that of Adam.[5] Theodore compares the teaching of the prophet Ezekiel with that of St. Paul to show that God does not punish one man for another's sake, but that every man will have to give account for his own offences.[6] The truth of individual moral responsibility can be upheld without denying that men do suffer because of the sins of others, and for their sakes, which is the essence of the doctrine of vicarious suffering.

It would be more in accordance with Theodore's

---

[1] Rom. v. 13.
[2] *Ib.* v. 18.
[3] *Orig. Sin*, bk. iii, fr. 3.
[4] *Ib.* fr. 3.
[5] Rom. v. 13.
[6] *Orig. Sin*, bk. iii, fr. 3.

THE DOCTRINE OF MAN

conception of man to say that sin was the consequence of mortality than that it was its cause. Since we are mortal according to the present life, mortality has somehow as its consequence a readiness to sin.[1] The flesh, which denotes human nature in its weakness and mortality, is liable to give way to natural desires and so to sin.[2]

However, these natural defects have their compensations. Mortality itself may be regarded, from one aspect, as a blessing in disguise. God made us mortal in this present life, because He wished to bring us to the perfection of goodness.[3] This life is intended by God to be a training ground in virtue.[4]

Theodore does not believe in the original perfection of man, and his subsequent perversion, but in his natural imperfection and the ultimate perfectibility of human nature. On this point he agrees with the teaching of earlier theologians. Theophilus of Antioch asserted that " Adam was still an infant (νήπιος), and therefore he could not receive knowledge worthily."[5] Clement of Alexandria seems to attribute to man physical, but not mental or moral perfection. " Adam was perfect, as regards his formation."[6] And yet " he was not created perfect, but only in a condition to attain perfection."[7]

---

[1] Eph. ii. 10, iv. 22 (Swete, vol. i, pp. 147, 173), Col. iii. 4 (" Sin is a consequence of mortality ").
[2] Rom. vii. 5, xiii. 14, Gal. ii. 15, v. 13.
[3] Rom. ix. 15.
[4] Gal. ii. 15.
[5] Theophilus, *op. cit.* bk. ii, chap. xxv.
[6] Clem. Alex. *Strom.* iv, chap. xxiii.
[7] *Ib.* vi, chap. xii (Gore, *Belief in Christ*, p. 274).

Still these natural and inherent defects do not amount to total depravity. It is generally admitted that man is an amalgam of good and evil. Even Tertullian, who argues that there is an antecedent " vitium originis," insists that there is the principal, divine, and truly natural good inherent in the soul. This is the proper basis of moral responsibility. " On this account no soul is without guilt, because none is without the seed of good." [1] Tertullian, as a Traducianist, held that the good and evil qualities of the soul were inherited by the child from its parents. Creationists, on the other hand, would be obliged to argue that evil was inherited through the body alone.[2] As far as we are able to judge, Theodore was slightly in favour of the Traducian view.[3] However, our inclination to evil does not obscure our knowledge of good. " Though we happen to have a powerful inclination to the worse, yet we have a sure knowledge of good in the soul, and there is no man, who does not know at all what is better in life." [4]

Again, Theodore declares categorically that sin

---

[1] Tertullian, *de Anima*, xli. He was deeply influenced by the psychology of the Stoics. The soul has a corporeal nature (*de Anima*, v) and soul and spirit are identical (x). So the Stoics affirmed that the soul is a body, or a warm breath ($\pi\nu\epsilon\hat{\upsilon}\mu\alpha$) pervading the whole body (Adam, *Texts to illustrate Philosophy after Aristotle*, p. 40).

[2] *Cp*. Bethune-Baker, *Introduction to Early History of Christian Doctrine*, p. 303.

[3] While he maintained the close connexion of soul and body in the individual, he asserted that the soul and body were separated by sin (Rom. viii. 19).

[4] Rom. ix. 15.

THE DOCTRINE OF MAN 19

is not a property of the nature, but of the will.[1] The distinction made between nature and will is useful and important. Nature means, no doubt, the sum of instincts which are inherited by us from our parents and transmitted from our primeval ancestors. The questions of heredity and instinct cannot be fully discussed at this point, but we may accept the definition of instinct as an " innate specific tendency of the mind that is common to all members of any species."[2] The instincts, therefore, are the necessary endowment of every human being. They are primitive and powerful, but they are in themselves neutral. A tendency to action, however strong, is not synonymous with an act or a habit, and it is only these which can be strictly termed sinful.[3]

The source of sin, then, is the will. Yet that faculty is not inexorably determined by motives or impulses, but is freely exercised within certain limits of outward circumstances and inward disposition.[4] The freedom of the will is the strongest point in the ethical system of the school of Antioch. Theophilus regarded this as the essential characteristic of human personality. " God made man free and self-determining."[5] This was the soundest and most valuable element in the doctrinal system

---

[1] *Orig. Sin*, bk. iii, fr. 3.

[2] McDougall, *Introduction to Social Psychology* (1920), p. 22, quoted by Tansley, *The New Psychology*, p. 34. Perhaps it is better to speak of instinct as " a tendency to action."

[3] *Cp.* Bicknell, *Theological Introduction to the Thirty-nine Articles*, pp. 232, 233.

[4] Bicknell, *op. cit.* p. 240.

[5] Theophilus, *op. cit.* bk. ii, chap. xxvii.

of Paul of Samosata.[1] Chrysostom, who endeavoured to overcome the easy-going fatalism and moral apathy which prevailed in his day at Constantinople, was never weary of emphasizing the freedom of man's will and the power of self-determination.[2] It is the moral purpose ($\pi\rho o\alpha i\rho\epsilon\sigma\iota s$) which is perverted when men sin.[3]

Theodore argues that man must have free-will because he is a rational being. "On every side our reasoning faculty and power of choice is exercised in us."[4] That power was given to us, but, of course, it is often misused. "The power of choosing the good or the worse is in our hands,"[5] but "it is not just to abuse this freedom by sinning."[6] Though the strength of natural impulse or acquired habit ought not to be underrated, the will is still free to yield to temptation or to strive against sin. Besides this, it can be assisted by or resist Divine grace.

While the theologians of the school of Antioch asserted the fact of man's free-will, they did not deny the need of God's grace. Grace can be defined in the words of St. Paul as "God working in us." It is the action of the Divine will upon the human

---

[1] *Cp.* Dr. Kidd, *History of the Church*, bk. i, p. 502. "There is something morally fine and noble about the system of Paul, because of the value which he attached to personal effort and the power of the will."

[2] Chrys. *Hom. in Gen.* xx. 3, *in Matt.* lix. 1, 2, *in Rom.* xix. 1, 5.

[3] Ib. *Hom. in Rom.* xii. 6. The term $\pi\rho o\alpha i\rho\epsilon\sigma\iota s$ is used by Plato (*Parmenides*, 143C), and Aristotle (*Eth. Nic.* bk. iii). The latter defines it as a deliberate desire for what is in our power.

[4] Gal. ii. 15. [5] Rom. ix. 14. [6] Gal. v. 13.

THE DOCTRINE OF MAN 21

soul. We cannot do good works without God's grace. " What we were unable to achieve by our own purpose, we could accomplish by the grace of Him, who regenerated us to this end."[1]

Nevertheless, Chrysostom and Theodore differ from Augustine in laying the chief stress not on prevenient but on co-operating grace. Chrysostom affirms emphatically that " God does not anticipate our volitions : but when we take the initiative and exercise our will, then He also gives us many means of salvation."[2]

Theodore, indeed, seems to postulate an initial act of God at the beginning of our spiritual life, presumably at our baptism. God called us, and gave us the grace of the Holy Spirit. But it is our work to remain firm in the faith. That was our contribution to the work of salvation ; the remaining benefits accrued from His grace.[3] If we exercise our own wills, we are sure to find God's grace co-operating with us. His co-operation is necessary, that we may think and do what is pleasing to Him.[4] We can understand why Theodore supported the positive teaching of Pelagius and Julian of Eclanum as to free-will and grace, while he avoided the extreme exaggerations of their doctrine. It is difficult and perhaps dangerous to dogmatize too confidently about the methods and limits of God's

[1] Theodore, Eph. ii. 10.
[2] Chrys. *Hom. in Joann.* xviii. 3. Cp. *Hom. in Eph.* iv. 2. " Since God willed, faith saved. No one is justified by works, that the grace and kindness of God might be manifested."
[3] Theodore, Gal. v. 8. [4] Phil. ii. 13.

action upon the human soul, but we believe that Theodore tried to do justice to both aspects of the truth, by affirming the real, though relative, freedom of man, and the inspiring but not irresistible grace of God.[1]

[1] *Cp.* W. R. Sorley, *Moral Values and the Idea of God*, pp. 494, 495. "In meeting and welcoming the divine grace, man's spirit is not passive but responsive.... The Spirit of God is conceived as working in and through the spirit of man, but in such a way as not to destroy human freedom."

CHAPTER III

THE DOCTRINE OF GOD AND CHRIST

THE anthropology of Theodore leads on directly to his Christology, with which it is closely connected. But before discussing his view of the Incarnation, it would be desirable to examine his general doctrine of God.

It is the fundamental principle of Christian theology, as expounded in the schools of Alexandria and Antioch, that God is a purely spiritual being. This conception was based on the progressive revelation of God given to the Hebrew prophets and the positive teaching of the New Testament, especially of our Lord. At the same time the Church fathers were probably influenced to some extent by Platonic idealism. The teaching of Origen bears a close correspondence to that of Theodore, and may be compared in its main features. Origen declared that God is unseen and incorporeal,[1] not limited by a bodily form,[2] and immutable in substance.[3] Theodore's view is almost identical, and can be described in its broad outlines.

God is incorporeal. This fact was clearly demonstrated by our Lord's conversation with the Samari-

---
[1] Orig. *contra Cels.* vii. 38. Cp. *de Princ.* i. 1.
[2] *On Prayer*, xxiii.　　　　[3] *Contra Cels.* iv. 14.

tan woman.[1] We offer Him, therefore, not a fleshly but a spiritual worship, because He is Spirit.

It follows that He is unlimited in nature.[2] He is in all things with the fulness of His Godhead, and transcends the whole creation.

As Spirit, God is invisible to us by nature,[3] but He has manifested Himself through His Son. Christ is the visible image of the invisible God.[4]

Once more, God is immutable.[5] This quality of the Divine being is most vigorously maintained by the Eastern theologians. They shrank naturally from any suggestion of pagan metamorphosis, and, on that ground, were firmly opposed to Arianism with its theory of a changeable Godhead. The general statement of the Eastern theologians is doubtless correct, but needs some slight qualification to avoid misconception. God cannot change in His essential nature, but He does change, apparently, in His relation to man. The moral change, which is presupposed by Divine forgiveness, takes place rather in man than in God. But this point must be more fully considered when we discuss the question of the Incarnation.

Before passing on to this question, we must briefly refer to Theodore's teaching about the Holy Trinity.

Theodore believes in one Divine substance re-

[1] *Cp*. Phil. iii. 3, 2 Cor. iii. 17.
[2] Eph. i. 22, 23, *de Incarn.* bk. vii. ($\dot{a}\pi\epsilon\rho\iota\gamma\rho\alpha\phi$os $\tau\dot{\eta}\nu$ $\phi\dot{\upsilon}\sigma\iota\nu$).
[3] 1 Tim. vi. 16.
[4] Col. i. 15.
[5] 1 Tim. i. 11, *cp*. vi. 15, where this point is made clear in the Latin version.

THE DOCTRINE OF GOD AND CHRIST 25

vealed in three persons. This view is clearly expressed in three passages. In the first he says, "Our confession of the Godhead is inseparable. Our conceptions (γνῶμαι) are not divided according to the number of the persons (πρόσωπα), but we worship them alike."[1] A fuller statement is made by him in the Ecthesis. "We confess that the Father is perfect in person (πρόσωπον), and the Son likewise, and the Spirit in the same manner. The principle of piety is safeguarded by us in not thinking that Father, Son, and likewise Holy Spirit are different substances (οὐσίαι), but one, which is acknowledged in identity of Godhead."[2] Lastly, a letter written by Theodore to Artemius, priest of Alexandria, has been preserved for us by Facundus. This declares that "we worship Father, Son, and Holy Spirit. . . . Each one of these is of the same substance (essentia). So we speak of three persons (personæ), thinking each to be perfect and of the same substance ; and we worship three persons, believing them to be of one truly Divine substance."[3]

Theodore appears to prefer the term πρόσωπον to the term ὑπόστασις in expressing his belief in the Holy Trinity. The former meant for him, probably, a particular form of manifestation of the one Divine being, while the latter was applied to the distinct existence of God or man. The term πρόσωπον had been discredited by Sabellius, who used it in the

[1] Eph. iv. 6.
[2] Ecthesis (Swete, vol. ii, p. 328).
[3] To Artemius, *Ep.* ii. (Swete, vol. ii, p. 338).

sense of a merely temporary aspect or function. But there is no reason why it should not be taken to mean an eternal and essential form or mode of being, and so it would become the equivalent of ὑπόστασις.[1] Some term was obviously needed that would imply a real distinction in the being of God without suggesting that there were three separate individuals. It must somehow be a mean between individual and aspect. It may be doubted whether either πρόσωπον or ὑπόστασις were as concrete entities as person in the modern sense. Perhaps there is no exact agreement as to the nature of human personality at the present time. Though it cannot be entirely isolated and impermeable, yet it is a definite and distinct subject. But, even if the nature of human personality could be closely determined, it would be unwise to press the analogy between human and Divine personality beyond certain limits. After all, the most perfect analogy does not amount to complete correspondence. The same problem must be faced with regard to the relations of God and man in the Incarnation.

In dealing with this question, we propose to take our starting-point from the manhood of Christ and move upwards to His Godhead. This was also the method adopted by most of the leaders of the school of Antioch.

---

[1] *Cp.* Bethune-Baker, *op. cit.* pp. 234, 237. Basil of Cæsarea (*Epp.* 38, 214) defined ὑπόστασις as a particular mode of being (οὐσία). Theodoret accepts this definition, and argues that ὑπόστασις and πρόσωπον are equivalent terms (*Eranistes*, dial. i. § 8).

THE DOCTRINE OF GOD AND CHRIST 27

Generally speaking, Theodore held that Christ came to restore the unity of the world which had been broken by man's sin, and to raise man by union with Himself to a condition of perfect freedom from sin and death. To fulfil this purpose, the Word must become man, and pass through all the experiences of human life.

Christ, then, was true and perfect man. He was not a mere man, as Paul of Samosata and others falsely alleged,[1] but truly and fully man.[2] He assumed flesh and a soul, immortal and endowed with reason.[3]

Theodore followed his predecessors in the school of Antioch by maintaining the complete manhood of our Lord. Eustathius and Diodore had attacked the Arians for denying that our Lord had a human soul.[4] In particular, Theodore condemned the theory of Apollinarius, that the Logos took the place of the rational soul. He argued that if the Godhead had taken the place of the human reason, the man Jesus would not have felt fear, or wrestled in prayer, or needed the help of the Holy Spirit.[5] If He had no human soul, the temptations would have been a mere dramatic display.[6] This would

---

[1] *De Apoll.* bk. iii, fr. 12, *On the Mysteries*, bk. xiii.
[2] *De Incarn.* bk. vi, bk. xiii. fr. 3.
[3] *Ib.* bk. xv, fr. 3, *de Apoll.* bk. iii. fr. 10, and Ecthesis (Swete, vol. ii, p. 329).
[4] Eustathius, *de Anima* (*ap.* Theodt. *Eranistes*, dial. i. § 56 and dial. iii. § 234) ; Diodore on Pss. 71 v. 23, 72 v. 5 (*ap.* Mai, *Bibl. nova patrum*, vol. vi, p. 248).
[5] *De Apoll.* bk. vi, frs. 4 and 7.
[6] *De Incarn.* bk. xv, fr. 3.

reduce the spiritual life of our Lord to a Docetic illusion.

But Christ passed through all the human experiences, both of body and soul. He hungered, thirsted, and suffered like all other men.[1] From His earliest childhood, He went through a real physical and mental development.[2] He was tempted like us, yet without sin. Theodore describes our Lord's temptations in the wilderness,[3] but he asserts that the spiritual temptations, by which no doubt are meant the temptations to pride and ambition, were more difficult to overcome than the temptations of the flesh.[4] Again, He endured a real mental conflict at Gethsemane, and that of no ordinary kind.[5]

It is a necessary presupposition from these facts that our Lord, as man, possessed a free will. Theodore insists very strongly on this point. We must not say that the man had no purpose ($\pi\rho\delta\theta\epsilon\sigma\iota\varsigma$) of his own: nay more, so far as it was compatible with free purpose, there was added to him the love of good and the hatred of evil. The integrity of his purpose was preserved by Divine grace, or by the co-operation of the Word.[6] These were indispensable conditions of His moral progress in the course of His earthly life. He advanced in wisdom and favour with God and men,[7] because the Divine Word afforded His co-operation for the successful accomplishment of duty and the complete attain-

---

[1] *De Incarn.* bk. vii, *ad baptizandos*, lect. viii.
[2] *Ib.*
[3] *Ib.* bk. xiii, fr. 2.
[4] *Ib.* bk. xv, fr. 3.
[5] *Ib.* bk. x, fr. 2.
[6] *Ib.* bk. vii, bk. xiv, fr. 2.
[7] Luke ii. 52.

THE DOCTRINE OF GOD AND CHRIST 29

ment of virtue.[1] Theodore bases this argument in the first place on the explicit language of St. Luke, but he may have been influenced to some extent by the ethical teaching of the Peripatetic school of philosophy. The Peripatetics taught that progress ($προκοπή$) was possible towards perfection in virtue.[2] This term was used by Paul of Samosata to express his belief in the moral progress of Christ,[3] and was probably inherited from him by the teachers of the school of Antioch.[4] They believed, if we understand them rightly, that perfection is not a static condition but a dynamic process. That does not mean that our Lord advanced, like the rest of men aspire to do, from imperfection to perfection, but rather that He was perfect at every stage of His human life, from earliest infancy to mature manhood.

There were, as Theodore clearly points out, certain physical and spiritual conditions or causes of our Lord's human perfection.

First of all, there was the supernatural birth. Christ's unique discernment of good from His earliest youth was due to the fact that He was not born like other men from the copulation of a man and a woman, but was formed by the Divine operation of the Holy Spirit.[5] Theodore firmly believed in

---

[1] *De Incarn.* bk. vii.
[2] Diogenes Laertius, vii. 127.
[3] Paul of Samosata. Fragment xiii (*J.T.S.* vol. xix, pp. 20–41).
[4] *V.* Eustathius (Migne, *P.G.* vol. xviii, §§ 688, 694).
[5] *De Incarn.* bk. vii.

the Virgin birth,[1] but he shrank from calling the Blessed Virgin *Theotokos*, because he could not bring himself to say that God, as God, was begotten of the Virgin.[2] Strictly speaking, He that was born of the Virgin and of the substance of His mother was not God of God and of the substance of the Father, but the temple of God.[3] Still, Theodore was ready to go half-way to meet the criticism of opponents. If he were asked, " Was Mary the mother of man or mother of God ? " he would answer " Both " : one by the nature of the fact, the other by relation. She was the mother of man naturally, but she was also mother of God, since God was in the man that was born.[4] God the Word was not born in Himself, but rather incarnate.[5] This explanation did not, doubtless, satisfy opponents, who regarded it as an evasion of the issue. But, at any rate, Theodore was determined to maintain the real and vital distinction between the human and Divine natures.

Another condition of our Lord's holiness was the co-operation or indwelling of the Holy Spirit. As

---

[1] Fragment *de Incarn.* (Swete, vol. ii, p. 311), *de Apoll.* bk. iii, fr. 1. *Cp.* Ecthesis (Swete, vol. ii, p. 329).

[2] *De Apoll.* bk. iii, fr. 1.

[3] *Ib.* and *cp.* Eustathius (Theodt. *Eranistes*, dial. i. § 57), and Diodore (*P.G.* xxxiii. 1560B). Athanasius (*ad Epictetum*, chap. x) calls the body the temple of the Word, but he would have included the soul as part of the manhood (*Tomus ad Ant.* vii).

[4] *De Incarn.* bk. xv, fr. 2.

[5] *De Apoll.* bk. iii, fr. 1.

THE DOCTRINE OF GOD AND CHRIST 31

we have said before, He was formed by the Holy Spirit in the Virgin's womb. He was justified in the Spirit before His baptism because He kept the law with appropriate strictness.[1] Then, He was anointed by the Holy Spirit, who descended on Him at His baptism.[2] He was led by the Spirit into the wilderness, and strengthened for the right performance of His appointed task.[3] From first to last, the Spirit worked wholly in Him, and co-operated with Him in His life of grace.[4]

Although no hard and fast distinction is drawn between the operations of the Divine Word and the Holy Spirit, two points are sufficiently clear. Firstly, Theodore is not an Adoptianist in the ordinary sense of that term. He did not hold that Christ was adopted as the Son of God for the first time at His baptism, because he believed that He was conceived by the Holy Spirit in the Virgin's womb. If it be further urged that the man Christ Jesus was adopted at the first moment of conception,[5] then the same argument might be applied to the assumption of a human soul at any point of the Incarnation. Secondly, Theodore's objection to Apollinarianism is based on the ground that, if the

---

[1] *De Incarn.* bk. xiii, fr. 1. An alternative view is that this justification applies to His later life.

[2] *De Apoll.* bk. iii, fr. 7.

[3] *Ib.* fr. 6.

[4] *De Incarn.* bk. vii, *sub fine*, bk. xiii, fr. 1. *Cp.* 1 Tim. iii. 16.

[5] Gal. iv. 4, Col. i. 13. These two passages are interpreted by Theodore as referring to Christ as man. But they must also refer to the Incarnate Word.

Word took the place of the human reason, Christ would not have needed the co-operation of the Holy Spirit for justification, or conquering the devil, or the rest of His self-manifestation in life and work.[1] Therefore, the real and complete manhood of Christ was needed for the continuous indwelling of the Holy Spirit.

But, above all, the chief cause of His human perfection was His union with the Divine Word. This union was preserved throughout His earthly life and increased progressively until it was finally revealed and consummated by the Resurrection and Ascension. Then He became impassible and immutable both in body and soul, and sits now at the right hand of God to judge the whole world.[2] So He remains true and perfect man even in His glorified and eternal state.

How, then, was the union of the man with the Divine Word to be conceived?

Theodore uses the ideas which have been already put forward by his predecessors in the school of Antioch, but he expresses them to some extent in a fresh and original manner.

First there is the familiar idea of assumption. This term or conception was common both to the schools of Alexandria and Antioch. Origen expresses himself in clear and definite language. " The

[1] *De Apollin.* bk. iii, frs. 7, 11.

[2] *Ib.* bk. iii, fr. 10; Catechetical Lectures (Swete, vol. ii, p. 326). "He (the Word) making him (the man) incorruptible and immortal and immutable led him to heaven." Eph. i. 10. "He made the body incorruptible and impassible, and restored it to the immortality of His soul."

THE DOCTRINE OF GOD AND CHRIST

immortal God-Word assumed a mortal body and a human soul."[1] Athanasius, too, asserts that "the Word took upon Him our flesh, and assumed a body like ours."[2] On the other hand, Diodore and Chrysostom employed the same term, each in his characteristic manner. Diodore's language is terse and antithetical. "The Son of God assumed the son of David."[3] Chrysostom affirms clearly that the Word was God, and took manhood, consisting of body and soul.[4] Theodore's language resembles most closely that of Origen. "God the Word assumed a perfect man, consisting of a rational soul and human flesh,"[5] or, if we look at the matter from the human side, "the man was assumed by the Only-begotten Son."[6]

Theodore insists strongly on the difference of the Divine and human natures and the inequality which exists between Him that assumes and him who is assumed.[7] Yet, while the distinction is maintained, the unity is most emphatically asserted. "He that assumes is not that which is assumed, nor that which is assumed He that assumes. But the unity of the assumed with Him that assumes is inseparable, and incapable of severance in any respect."[8] It is unnecessary to multiply quotations, as these

---

[1] Orig. *contra Cels.* bk. iv. 5.
[2] Athan. *Or. contr. Arianos*, ii. 7, *et al.*
[3] Diodore (Migne, *P.G.* xxxiii. 1560A).
[4] Chrys. *Hom. in Phil.* vii.
[5] Ecthesis (Swete, vol. ii, p. 328).
[6] *De Apollin.* bk. iv, fr. 4.
[7] *Ib.* bk. iv, frs. 3–5; *de Incarn.* bk. v.
[8] *De Apollin.* bk. iv, fr. 1.

THEODORE OF MOPSUESTIA

correlative terms denoting the Godhead and manhood of the Incarnate Christ occur almost on every page of Theodore's extant works on Christian doctrine.

Again, Theodore employs the term which was current in the church of Antioch since the middle of the third century, namely, συνάφεια. It does not denote an accidental association, but a close cohesion or union.[1]

The term appears to have been introduced into theology by Paul of Samosata. He wished to describe an intimate but voluntary union between the man Jesus and God. " The Saviour was united (συναφθείς) with God, and never admits of any separation for all eternity, because He has one and the same will with Him."[2] Paul does not discriminate between the terms συνάφεια or ἕνωσις, but he adheres to the voluntary union as the only possible method between different natures and different persons or modes of being (πρόσωπα).[3]

The term συνάφεια is not found in the extant fragments of Eustathius or Diodore, but it reappears in those of Flavian, Bishop of Antioch in A.D. 381. He declares that the union (συνάφεια) is not to be conceived in a physical manner,[4] and that the human nature is united to the Godhead, though each nature remains by itself.[5]

---

[1] *Cp.* Bethune-Baker, *Nestorius and his Teaching*, p. 90.
[2] *J.T.S.* vol. xix. p. 39 f. Fragments xiii, xv, xvii.
[3] *Ib.* frs. xi, xii.
[4] *Ap.* Theodt. *Eranistes*, dial. i. § 66.
[5] *Ib.* dial. iii. § 161.

THE DOCTRINE OF GOD AND CHRIST 35

Chrysostom, again, combines the two terms ἕνωσις and συνάφεια in speaking of the Incarnation, and evidently recognizes no difference between them.[1] But he is strongly opposed to any confusion (σύγχυσις) of substances or natures.

In the same way, Theodore is quite impartial in his use of the two terms in various forms. Συνάφεια occurs most frequently in the Ecthesis,[2] and is doubtless represented by the Latin words *copulatio* or *conjunctio*, which are found in the commentary on the Epistles and elsewhere.[3]

At one time Theodore regards the union from the Divine side, at other times from the human side. The God-Word united the man with Himself.[4] On the other hand, the man has an inseparable union with the Divine nature, and shares in the unique privileges of Sonship by his union with the God-Word.[5]

Theodore, like Chrysostom, wished to affirm the closest and most intimate union, and yet to avoid the suggestion of any mixture or confusion of the Divine and human natures.[6] " The theory of mixture," he says, " is superfluous and improper and

[1] *Hom. in Joann.* xi, cp. xxxv iii. and *Hom. in Phil.* vii, chap. 3.
[2] Swete, vol. ii, pp. 329, 330.
[3] Phil. ii. 11, Col. i. 15 ; *de Apollin.* iii. frs. 3, 8, and Swete, vol. ii, p. 326. The word *adunatio* is frequently used in the same sense.
[4] Ecthesis (Swete, vol. ii, p. 329), cp. *de Incarn.* xiv, fr. 2.
[5] Ecthesis (Swete, vol. ii, pp. 329, 330), *cp.* Catechet. Lect. (p. 324).
[6] Origen uses the terms κρᾶσις or ἀνάκρασις (*contra Cels.* iii. 41, *de Princ.* ii. 6). Apollinarius, Gregory Nazianzen, and Gregory of Nyssa employ the term μίξις or various compounds of κρᾶσις (*v.* C. E. Raven, *Apollinarianism*, pp. 259, 266).

36 THEODORE OF MOPSUESTIA

inharmonious, as each of the natures remains indissolubly by itself, but the theory of union (ἕνωσις) is clearly harmonious."[1]

So long as the distinction between the Divine and human natures is maintained, Theodore is indifferent to the use of the terms συνάφεια or ἕνωσις. What really matters to him is the mode of conceiving the union. Writing to Domnus, who was afterwards Bishop of Antioch (440-452), Theodore rejects the idea of a substantial union, and accepts that of a voluntary union. "The thought of a substantial union is true only with elements of the same substance, but with elements of a different substance it is false, because it cannot be pure from confusion: but the mode of union by good-will (εὐδοκία) preserves the natures unconfused, and shows that the person (πρόσωπον) made up of both is one and indivisible."[2]

A third theory of union, which Theodore expounds with the greatest clearness, is that of indwelling (ἐνοίκησις). It had been propounded in one form or another by the earlier teachers of the school of Antioch. Eustathius said that the man was the temple, in which God dwelt.[3] Diodore affirmed that the God-Word, existing before the ages, dwelt in him of the seed of David.[4] Chrysostom was anxious to maintain that, whether it was the Son or the Word, there dwelt in Him not a

[1] *De Incarn.* bk. viii.
[2] Letter to Domnus (Swete, vol. ii, p. 338).
[3] Theodt. *Eranistes*, dial. i. § 57, ii. § 134.
[4] Diodore (*P.G.* xxxiii. 1560A).

THE DOCTRINE OF GOD AND CHRIST 37

sort of activity (ἐνέργεια), but a substance (οὐσία).[1]

This theory of indwelling is most fully and carefully defined by Theodore. He discusses three modes of indwelling, by substance (οὐσία), by activity or operation (ἐνέργεια), and by good-will (εὐδοκία).[2]

First of all, the idea that God dwells in men by substance is discussed and rejected. On the one hand, it is clear that God does not dwell in all, but only in His saints, and those who are fitted for communion with Him. On the other hand, it is improper and absurd to limit His substance, as His infinite nature is everywhere present and limited at no point of space.[3]

The same objection is urged against the idea of God's indwelling by operation. Either the operation of God must be limited to the saints, (and yet God's providence and government are extended to all His works,) or all must have a share in His operation, because all things are empowered by Him for their subsistence and natural activity. But it has been already denied that God dwells in all.

Only one other mode remains, that He dwells in man by good-will (εὐδοκία). This term has been most unfortunately rendered by the word complacency, which suggests a sort of patronizing conde-

[1] Chrys. *Hom. in Col.* iii, cp. *Hom.* vi.
[2] *De Incarn.* bk. vii.
[3] Cp. *de Incarn.* bk. ix, fr. 3. God is everywhere by nature, but He acts by His mind. So Diodore (on Ps. 73^{26}) says, "No one is separated from God by space, but the unrighteous man is conceived as being far from the righteous God by disposition."

scension on the part of the Almighty. Theodore explains that good-will means the best and noblest will ($\theta\acute{\epsilon}\lambda\eta\sigma\iota\varsigma$) of God, which He exercises towards "those who fear Him and hope in His mercy."[1] God's good-will and co-operation are conditioned partly by His own purpose and partly by the characters of men. It is true, in one sense, that God is present to all, because He is infinite and unlimited by nature. But He is near to some and far from others by good-will and spiritual affinity.

To sum up, God effects His indwelling by good-will, not limiting His substance or operation to some, and being separated from the rest, but being present to all in substance, yet separated from those who are unworthy by the state of their disposition.

When Theodore compares the indwelling of God in righteous men and the indwelling of the Word in the man Jesus, he declares that the mode is the same, but the degree is different. God dwells in the apostles and righteous men by good-will, but He dwells in Christ as "in a Son." What does that mean? It means that He (the Word) dwelt in him and united the whole of him that was assumed to Himself, and prepared him to partake with Him of all the honour, of which He Himself being Son by nature and dwelling in him partakes. The difference between the indwelling of God in all other men and

[1] Ps. cxlvii. 11. As the will seems to be the predominant factor, I cannot quite agree with Dr. Raven, who renders $\epsilon\dot{\upsilon}\delta o\kappa\acute{\iota}a$ as "love in action" or "love expressed by will" (*Apollinarianism*, p. 302). Yet the difference is not fundamental, because the Divine will must be a loving will, and love must be shown in action.

THE DOCTRINE OF GOD AND CHRIST 39

in Christ was so great as to be not merely a difference in degree but a difference in kind.

Again, there was another specific difference between the indwelling of the Word in Christ and in other men. The Word was in the man from the very first moment of conception.[1] The indwelling must be carried back to the very first moment of the human existence of Christ. The man was united with the Word at his formation in the womb.[2] It would be difficult to think of a union more original and absolute than this.

The mode of union leads us on to the crucial question, did Theodore believe in the unity of our Lord's incarnate Person? There seems to be no doubt that he did, though the expression of his belief may sometimes be ambiguous and unsatisfactory.

He affirms in many passages his belief in the distinction or difference of the Divine and human natures, and the unity of person.[3] These statements might seem to be clear and definite enough, but there is one important passage which needs careful investigation, because Theodore appears at first sight to teach that there were two persons combined into one person.

The passage runs as follows : " From all sides it is clear that the theory of mixture [4] is superfluous and improper and inharmonious, as each of the natures

[1] *De Apollin.* bk. iii, fr. 2.

[2] *De Incarn.* bk. vii, bk. xiii, fr. 3.

[3] *Ib.* bks. v, x, xi (persona), xii ($\pi\rho\delta\sigma\omega\pi o\nu$), xv (persona).

[4] Here Theodore is condemning Apollinarius and possibly others, like Gregory Nazianzen or Gregory of Nyssa.

remains indissolubly by itself, but the theory of union (ἕνωσις) is clearly harmonious. For through this the natures are brought together and make up one person (πρόσωπον) by union. What the Lord says about the man and the woman, ' so they are no longer two but one flesh,'[1] we would naturally say regarding the union, so they are no longer two persons but one, the natures being clearly discriminated. In the former case, we do not, by speaking of one flesh, do violence to the number of two, for it is clear in what respect they are called one: so in the latter case the union of person does not do violence to the difference of natures. For when we distinguish the natures, we say that the nature of God the Word is complete, for it is not possible to speak of an impersonal substance (ἀπρόσωπο ὑπόστασις), and in like manner the nature of the man and his person is complete: but when we look at the union (συνάφεια), then we say one person (πρόσωπον)."[2] Theodore goes on to say that "the being (οὐσία) of God the Word is individual (ἰδία), and that of the man is individual, ... but when we look at the union (ἕνωσις), then we declare that there is one person of both natures."[3]

How is this passage to be explained? At any rate, it must be premised that Theodore believed

[1] Matt. xix. 6.
[2] *De Incarn.* bk. viii.
[3] Οὐσία may either be taken in the Platonic sense of abstract, universal, being or in the Aristotelian sense of concrete, individual, being (Dr. Kidd, *History of the Church*, vol. ii, p. 34). The latter seems more appropriate here.

THE DOCTRINE OF GOD AND CHRIST

that our Lord was perfect God and perfect man. On the one hand, he lays special emphasis on the personality of the Godhead, and denies that the Word has an impersonal existence, as Paul of Samosata taught : on the other hand, he refuses to say that the manhood was impersonal, which was the doctrine attributed to Apollinarius. But how can two persons become one person ? Theodore's analogy from the relations of husband and wife is not very apposite, because it is obvious that they remain separate individuals after matrimony.[1] At best it is only a moral union. Theodore seems to have realized that this was an imperfect analogy, because in his later treatise against Apollinarius he employs the illustration of soul and body. Soul and body are two distinct natures, and yet they make up one man.[2] We ought not to confound the natures, in order to preserve the unity of the two. Though they are united, the distinction of natures remains. Soul is one thing, and flesh another : one is immortal, and the other mortal. So in the Lord Christ the form of a servant exists in the form of God ; the unity of that which was assumed with Him that assumed is inseparable, and cannot be broken in any way. Of one thing Theodore is perfectly certain, that the distinction of natures does not destroy the unity of person.

[1] *Cp.* Catechetical Lectures, viii. "They remain two so far as they are two, and one so far as they are one."

[2] *De Apollin.* bk. iv, fr. 1. On the other hand, some things are one in nature, but different in person, as a human father and son. In the same way, the Divine Father and Son are One in Nature, but distinct in person (Catechetical Lectures, viii).

There may be, however, an alternative explanation of this passage in Theodore's treatise on the Incarnation, especially as regards the term πρόσωπον. This may mean the outward appearance or form of manifestation, rather than personality in the modern sense of a separate, self-conscious individual. Theodore speaks often of the form of a servant and the form of God, as in the treatise against Apollinarius. It is obvious that he has in his mind the second chapter of St. Paul's Epistle to the Philippians. Perhaps it may be useful to give a brief paraphrase of Theodore's commentary on this passage.[1]

St. Paul, he says, begins by speaking of Christ Jesus as of one person. Then he (St. Paul) mentions the two natures by distinguishing the form of God from the form of a servant. The words "being in the form of God" are understood of the person of Christ, while "the form of a servant" can be applied only to Christ because this was taken by Him. The phrase "that Jesus Christ is Lord" shows clearly that the man assumed is none else but Christ, and yet the difference of the natures is indicated by the properties ascribed to each. In speaking entirely about one person, he makes the union quite clear. In fact, in the whole of his argument about Christ, he speaks generally as of one person ; and sums up the different properties, that he may preserve the inseparable unity of the person. It seems clear from this exposition of St. Paul's argument that Theodore believed that the natures or forms, Divine

[1] Phil. ii. 5-11, *cp*. Col. i. 17 (commentary referring to Phil. ii).

THE DOCTRINE OF GOD AND CHRIST 43

and human, were united in one incarnate person. Or to put this statement in another way, the form of God and the form of man were united in one incarnate form, which was manifested to the world as one Christ.

Again, Theodore repudiated the charge of teaching that there were two Sons. Commenting on the first verse of the Epistle to the Hebrews, Theodore says that the true Son is He who possessed the Sonship by natural generation: but secondarily he also is included who truly partakes of the dignity by his union with Him. But yet we do not speak of two sons. " One son is rightly confessed since the distinction of natures ought necessarily to remain, and the union of person ought to be inseparably preserved."[1] Though he admits that the man has a unique sonship beyond the rest of men, through his union with the Word, he does not think that the man has a separate existence.

Again, if each were son and Lord according to substance, they could in some way be two sons and two Lords, according to the number of the persons. Since, however, one exists as Son and Lord according to substance, but the other is not reckoned as son or Lord according to his own being but, by union with Him, is known to share in the same qualities, on that account we speak of one Son and Lord.[2]

Theodore repeats this argument in the Ecthesis.[3]

---

[1] *De Incarn.* bk. xii, fr. 2; *cp.* however, fr. 7, where Theodore seems to postulate an independent human sonship.

[2] Catechetical Lectures, viii.

[3] Swete, vol. ii, pp. 329, 330.

There is one Son according to substance, God the Word. He that was assumed is jointly referred to by the name and with the honour of Son and Lord. He is not, like each one of us, son in himself—whence we are called "many sons" according to blessed Paul.[1] But he alone has this special privilege by his union with God the Word.

Theodore's argument about the two natures may not appear convincing to some minds, but evidently he believed that the Son of God and the man were united in one incarnate Person. He shrank, on the one hand, from asserting that the human nature was impersonal, or, at least, had no individual form and $πρόσωπον$.[2] On the other hand, he did not believe that the manhood existed independently as a separate being. Briefly, the man was distinct from the Word, but had no separate existence or personality.[3]

A similar problem had to be faced with regard to the two wills in the incarnate Christ. Theodore demonstrates clearly in two passages of his work on the Incarnation that he believes in the reality of the

---

[1] Heb. ii. 10. Theodore accepts the tradition of the Pauline authorship.

[2] *Cp.* Gore, *Belief in Christ*, p. 224, "In the Gospels we feel that we have a picture of the Son of Man intensely individual and unmistakably personal in His manhood," and Mackintosh, *Doctrine of Person of Jesus Christ* (2nd edn.), p. 385, "Jesus, as man, was possessed of personal individuality."

[3] Mackintosh, *op. cit.* p. 387, "We are rightly told that the truth ... is this, that the humanity of our Lord had no independent personality," and Gore, *op. cit.* pp. 227-8, "We should deprecate the use of the phrase 'impersonal manhood.' All that this really means is that the manhood had no separate personality."

THE DOCTRINE OF GOD AND CHRIST 45

human will of our Lord. It could not be said that our Lord, as man, had no purpose of his own. So far as was compatible with free purpose, there accrued to him the greatest love of good and hatred of evil. He had an extraordinary inclination to good by his union with God the Word, and received the co-operation of God the Word in conformity with his own purpose. The integrity of his purpose was preserved by divine grace, or by the co-operation of God the Word.[1] It seems clear from these passages that Theodore regards the human will as an active instrument in our Lord's incarnate life. The Divine Will does not completely absorb the human will, but co-operates with it.

However, in the later years of his life, Theodore writes to his friend Domnus and says: " The union of natures according to good-will effects of both natures one will, one operation. . . . He who was born from the Virgin's womb was united, as we say, by means of good-will to God the Word, and remained an indivisible temple (of the Word), having in all things the same will and operation as the Word Himself."[2] If Theodore had not abandoned his earlier convictions, it can only be supposed that he still believed in two wills, but in one personal action of the God-man. In the same way Cyril of Alexandria contrasts the human will with the Divine Will in describing our Lord's agony in Gethsemane, but he affirms in another connexion

---

[1] *De Incarn.* bk. vii, bk. xiv, fr. 2.
[2] Swete, *op. cit.* vol. ii, p. 338. Domnus was Bishop of Antioch (A.D. 440–452).

that there is one life-giving operation of Christ.[1] Without further evidence, we should not wish to accuse either Theodore or Cyril of Monothelitism. Even Nestorius says of our Lord's temptations, that "He raised his soul to God, conforming his volitions to those of God,"[2] and appears to have believed in a mutual interaction of the human and Divine wills.[3]

The problem was keenly debated in the seventh century, and the question was decided by the Sixth General Council, which declared that Christ had "two natural wills, not contrary one to the other, . . . but His human will follows . . . His divine and omnipotent will."[4] The distinction of the two wills is emphasized, but the union is not further explained. We hope to show later that a solution, so far as that is possible, must be sought on psychological lines. Still, Theodore and his contemporaries deserve credit for their courageous attempt to grapple with the problem of the two wills, as they were combined in our Lord's incarnate life.

[1] Cyril says of the raising of Jairus's daughter, Μία ζωόποιος ἐνέργεια Χριστοῦ—μίαν καὶ συγγενῆ δι' ἀμφοῖν ἐπιδείκνυσι τὴν ἐνέργειαν.

[2] Bethune-Baker, *Nestorius and his Teaching*, p. 127.

[3] *Ib.* p. 187. "For there was one and the same will and mind in the union of the natures, so that both should will and not will the same things. They (the natures) have, moreover, a mutual will."

[4] Hahn, *Symbole*, p. 173.

CHAPTER IV

SALVATION, THE CHURCH, AND THE SACRAMENTS

SALVATION can be viewed from two different standpoints, each of which is legitimate within its own sphere. Western theology represented the view that salvation consists in deliverance from sin: Eastern theology emphasized the idea that salvation implies the communication of life.[1]

As we might expect, Theodore takes the Eastern view of salvation. Sin is the consequence of mortality, and salvation consists in the transformation from mortality to immortality, the future state in which we shall be free from all sin. In this way the ideas of redemption and reconciliation are explained. "Christ was given as a redemption for us, who also delivered us from the power of death, and bestowed on us the hope of resurrection, with which we expect to live without all sin."[2] Theodore appears to draw a distinction between present redemption, which is deliverance from death, and final redemption, which will be freedom from all sin. So he says in another place that we have

---

[1] These two standpoints are represented in the New Testament by St. Paul and St. John.

[2] Eph. i. 7, *cp*. 13. Redemption will mean freedom from sin, intimate union with God, and participation in His glory.

redemption in Christ, for by Him we have obtained entire freedom from sins. But he adds this comment, that St. Paul "speaks of the future state, into which we shall be brought by the resurrection, and, as our nature will be immortal, we shall no longer be able to sin."[1] No doubt Theodore is right in pointing out that final salvation is a future ideal, but it remains none the less true that salvation is a process which begins in the present life.

In the same way reconciliation is conceived not so much in the sense of breaking down the barrier of sin as of union with Christ. "He reconciled all things in His death, and united things both in earth and heaven, in that He died and rose again; yea, by rising from the dead He gave to all the common promise of resurrection and immortality. All things are from this point knit together in concord, and look towards Him, as the author of concord."[2] Still, this union cannot be considered apart from sin. Man had been created to be the friendly bond of the whole creation, but this unity had been broken by sin. Christ, by rising again, and by reuniting His incorruptible body to His immortal soul, has, it seems, forged a link of friendship for the whole creation. However, this will be in the future life, when all men and the intelligible powers should look to Him, and keep enduring peace and concord with one another.[3] That is the summing-up, or restoration of all things in Christ. Again, it may be said that the reconciliation has been effected

[1] Col. i. 14.   [2] *Ib.* 20.   [3] Eph. i. 10.

SALVATION, CHURCH, AND SACRAMENTS 49

in this life, but will not be complete till the future life.

Theodore's doctrine of salvation seems to be determined by the general principle, that what is potential in the present state, will become actual in the future state.[1] At present all Christians stand midway between the two states of life.[2] Our spiritual progress depends on our right and proper use of the privileges and blessings provided in the Church and the Sacraments, which are the appointed means of salvation.

Theodore considers the Church from the main aspects familiar in the New Testament.

The Church is the body of Christ, and He is our Head. We, as members, are united and complete in Him.[3] Again, the Church is not only the body of Christ, but it is also the congregation of the faithful.[4] Theodore goes on to explain the words, " the fulness of Him, who is fulfilled in all," as meaning that " He is fully in all." God the Father or the Word is wholly in every individual because of the unlimitedness of His nature.[5] In the same way Christ is the Head of the Church, and the Church is the fulness of God, because He is in all and fills all.[6] Theodore interprets the words of St. Paul, " it pleased God that all the fulness should dwell

[1] Col. iii. 10.

[2] Gal. ii. 15.

[3] *Ib.* iii. 27 (*cp.* 1 Cor. xii. 27), Eph. v. 30.

[4] Eph. i. 23, *cp.* Article XIX, " The visible church of Christ is a congregation of faithful men."

[5] Cp. *De Incarn.* bk. vii.

[6] Col. i. 19.

in Him, that is Christ," as meaning that God vouchsafed to unite to Christ every creature that has been filled by Him. In the next chapter of this Epistle[1] Theodore takes "the fulness of the Godhead" to mean the whole creation filled by Him, because every creature dwells in, and has been united to Him. But it is obvious that St. Paul is thinking in the first place of the natural body in which God became incarnate, and not of Christ's mystical body, the Church.

Thirdly, the Church is the bride of Christ. He loves the Church as His own body, which has received her being and existence from Him. The Church is subject to Christ, as the wife to her husband.[2] Those who are not subject are no longer considered as belonging to the Church, because they have no sense of the body.

Lastly, Theodore points out clearly how we, the members of the Church, have been made the body of Christ. The Church has been made His body by spiritual regeneration, which has the form of the future resurrection.[3] Spiritual grace comes to us as from the Head, which is Christ. In each one of us a spiritual working is accomplished, which each one of us receives, and performs his function in the common organism. Christ builds up His own body because of the love which He bears to us, and we all have been made His body by spiritual regeneration.[4]

This spiritual regeneration is brought about by

[1] Col. ii. 9.
[2] Eph. v. 23 f.
[3] Col. i. 18.
[4] Eph. iv. 16.

SALVATION, CHURCH, AND SACRAMENTS 51

baptism. The beneficial effect of baptism is the joint work of Christ and the Holy Spirit.

The baptized receive the first-fruits of the Spirit and are regenerated.[1] He who does not receive baptism has not the Spirit, and participation in the Spirit is the cause and condition of all blessings either in this world or in the world to come.[2]

Again, they who have been baptized have put on Christ, that is, they have been united to Christ by the regeneration of baptism, and share in Christ's immortal nature.[3]

However, the idea which appeals most forcibly to Theodore and recurs most frequently in his discussion of St. Paul's teaching on this subject is that baptism is a type of the death and resurrection of Christ, which must be fulfilled in all Christians. Those who have been baptized have been crucified with Christ, and will rise like Him.[4] Or again, we are buried with Christ by baptism, so that, as the Lord rose from the dead, and entered a new life, we ourselves also are endowed with new life.[5]

Theodore repeats in many forms the same idea, that baptism is a type and pledge of our resurrection.[6] Our membership in the body of Christ is the

[1] Gal. ii. 16, Col. ii. 12, Eph. iv. 22.

[2] 1 Tim. iii. 6, 16, cp. *de Incarn.* bk. viii, where our baptism and participation of the Spirit is compared with our Lord's baptism.

[3] Rom. xiii. 14, Gal. iii. 27, *cp.* Col. i. 18 (commentary).

[4] Gal. ii. 20, *cp.* Rom. vi. 6.

[5] Rom. vi. 3, Col. ii. 12. *Cp.* the Collect for Easter Eve and the last prayer in Baptismal Service.

[6] Rom. vii. 4, Col. ii. 12, Eph. i. 22, 23, 1 Tim. i. 11.

assurance of our immortality. We are all members of Christ, who have received, through the regeneration of the Spirit, union with them in the hope of rising like Him.[1] Here, again, Theodore introduces the theory that Adam is the author of the present life, but Christ of the future life.[2] We are all one body according to the present life, because Adam is the head of the human race, and we are all of one nature. But in the future state, we shall all be one body, because we have received a common resurrection from Christ, who is our Head in the true order of things. In the same way, the remission of sins, which is connected with baptism, is a moral process which is completed in the future life. After we have become immortal in nature, we shall in no way be able to sin any more.[3]

It is interesting and instructive to note Theodore's view of infant baptism. There were various reasons for the postponement of baptism in the early ages of the Church. Many men were converts from heathenism, or, at least, had been brought up in a heathen environment. Others, no doubt, shrank from baptism, because there was only one repentance for deadly sins after baptism.[4] Apart from the extreme case of the Emperor Constantine, who was baptized on his deathbed, it is a well-known fact that Ambrose, Augustine, Jerome, Chrysostom,

[1] 1 Cor. vi. 15.
[2] Rom. vii. 4, Eph. i. 22, 23.
[3] Col. ii. 12, *cp*. 1 Tim. iii. 6, where the baptismal remission is asserted. So Photius (*bibl. Cod*. 177) attributes to Theodore the statement that there are two remissions of sins.
[4] Tertullian, *de Pœnitentia*, vii.

SALVATION, CHURCH, AND SACRAMENTS 53

and Theodore himself were not baptized till they had reached years of discretion.[1]

Theodore discusses the question of baptism from a logical and rational standpoint. He points out that the circumstances of baptism are often accidental. In one case a man receives the grace of baptism in his infancy through physical weakness: in another a man is baptized in extreme old age after a life of self-indulgence. The former may have lived a virtuous life, but fallen into some grave sins from time to time. It would be ridiculous that his generally virtuous life should not avail him at the last, because he had been baptized in infancy, while the latter should not suffer for his sins, but obtain glory in the future life, because he had been baptized at the end of his life on earth.

Theodore is arguing that baptism produces not a magical but a moral change, which should continue, in spite of occasional lapses, throughout the life of the individual. He quotes the further instances of Simon Magus and the penitent thief. Simon Magus was not helped by the gift of baptism, owing to his evil purpose, since the Holy Spirit did not rest on him; but the robber was not hindered from entering paradise because he had not received baptism.

Theodore does not wish to deny the effect or disparage the importance of baptism. It is a great privilege, because it comprises the bestowal of many blessings; and the purpose of each individual must

[1] Infant baptism did not become the common practice till the sixth century.

the mysteries are celebrated at all times.[1] Of course, it is right for the man who practises the greatest and most scandalous vices to abstain from the mysteries, because he who practises such things cannot inherit the Kingdom of God.[2] Those who commit lesser sins should take care to refrain from them as much as possible : and when they fall into such sins, it is not right to deprive them of the mysteries, but they should approach them with greater fear, considering their greatness. The benefits of communion are remission of sins and the co-operation of the Spirit. In fact, all that Christ has brought us by His death, is rightly accomplished by the symbols of His death. Theodore ventures to say that even if a man should happen to have sinned most grievously, but resolves to keep away from every unseemly action for the future, and to live in conformity to the laws of Christ, he should partake of the mysteries in full assurance of faith, and will receive pardon for all, and will by no means be disappointed in his confidence. Theodore attempts to steer a middle course between excessive laxity and rigorism. It is obviously undesirable to expose the sacred mysteries to the risk of irreverence and profanation, but it is also unwise to deter the grievously tempted but sincerely penitent sinner from using the means of grace which will give him the power to overcome

---

[1] Chrysostom witnesses to the practice of a daily Eucharist (*Hom. in Hebr.* xvii. 3. "Do we not offer every day ?")

[2] Theodore appears to recommend, even for such men, temporary but not permanent exclusion from communion.

SALVATION, CHURCH, AND SACRAMENTS

his sin. There is no very explicit reference in Theodore's works to any system of penance,[1] but he believes that the two great sacraments convey the remission of sins, which, however, can become final and complete only in the future life.

[1] *Cp.* however, a reference to public confession (ἐξομολόγησις) in Eph. i. 7. *V.* Swete's note *ad loc.*

CHAPTER V

THE LAST THINGS AND THE FUTURE LIFE

THEODORE's eschatology is based on the same general principle as his anthropology and his soteriology. There are two states of life, the present or mortal, and the future or immortal. Adam was the author of the former state, while the latter has been manifested by the second Adam, or Christ.[1]

The difference between the first and second Adam is indicated in many respects. The first began the former state, full of many evils; the second will bestow many blessings on us in the future state.[2] Again, as we all have been made in the likeness of Adam according to the present state, so we shall be made in the likeness of the Lord Christ hereafter. As we have been made partakers of the state of the first Adam, so we shall necessarily obtain a share in the future state of the second Adam, the Lord Christ. He took upon Himself the same human nature and all its properties, and endured death, that He might rise from the dead and make the nature free from death.[3]

---

[1] Ecthesis (Swete, vol. ii, p. 331).   [2] *Ib.*
[3] *Original Sin*, bk. iii, fr. 3. Theodore quotes Phil. iii. 21, 1 Cor. xv. 48, 49.

LAST THINGS AND FUTURE LIFE 59

In their present state of salvation, all Christians stand midway between the two states of life.[1] But the blessings which they now enjoy, such as regeneration and participation of the Spirit,[2] will be consummated by the second coming of Christ.

The Parousia is, so to speak, the event which will inaugurate our entrance into the new life. Christ will appear from heaven, and will bring us all into His own intimate fellowship and transform us into His own likeness.[3] Or again, when Christ, who is the author of our immortal life, appears, we also shall appear, and shall obtain the enjoyment of eternal life and future glory.[4] Once more, we look forward to all those blessings at the future time when our Lord Jesus Christ comes to judge the whole world.[5]

The judgment will manifest the working of the two natures of our Lord. He will appear as man, but will judge as God. We see that invisible nature in Him, because He has been united with God the Word and will judge the whole world.[6] The divine nature, which is invisible, will execute judgment in that man, who appears and is seen by all who are to be judged.[7] God will bestow rewards or inflict punishments in accordance with the actions of mankind. It does not matter whether their good deeds have been hidden from the knowledge of men, or, on the other hand, their sins have been manifest:

---

[1] Gal. ii. 15.
[2] *Ib.* iv. 24, 29.
[3] Ecthesis (Swete, vol. ii, p. 331).
[4] Col. iii. 4.
[5] 1 Thess. ii. 19.
[6] Col. i. 15.
[7] Acts xvii. 30, 31 (Ecthesis, Swete, vol. ii, p. 331).

they will, nevertheless, receive their due recompense.[1]

The general state of the blessed may be called salvation,[2] because that which is potential in the present life will become actual in the future life.[3] We have received remission of sins through the sacraments, but we shall obtain entire freedom from sins through the resurrection.[4] By the new creation and immortal life given to us by Christ, we were delivered from mortality and made free from every passion.[5] So we have been endowed with an immortal nature, in which we shall be incapable of sin.[6] Those who have been endowed with an immortal and impassible nature will no longer need the law for the attainment of virtue won by toil and effort, but their goodness will be preserved by Divine grace.[7] Theodore emphasizes in various ways the fact that the blessed will be free from corruption and sin.[8] Yet their happiness will consist not only in freedom from corruption and sin, but also in union and glory with God and Christ and all created beings.[9]

Furthermore, this salvation is not limited to those who have become members of the Church. It is true, as the Apostle says, that the dead in Christ shall rise first, but those who were righteous before the coming of Christ are not excluded from salva-

---

[1] 1 Tim. v. 24, 25.
[2] Eph. ii. 5.
[3] Col. iii. 10.
[4] *Ib.* i. 14.
[5] Eph. ii. 8.
[6] *Ib.* ii. 8, iv. 22.
[7] Phil. iii. 10.
[8] 1 Thess. iv. 7, Titus iii. 2.
[9] Col. i. 16, 2 Thess. i. 10–12.

LAST THINGS AND FUTURE LIFE 61

tion.[1] This belief is supported by the passage in the Epistle to the Hebrews concerning the patriarchs who trusted in God before the coming of Christ. "These all, being well reported through faith, did not obtain the promises, God having provided some better thing for us, that they might not be made perfect without us."[2] Since this was written after the coming of Christ, a distinction is made between the dead in Christ, that is those who believed in Christ and died for Christ's sake, and those who have not believed in Him. The righteous who had been before His coming, worked so far as lay in them, according to their time, and on that account will be rightly reckoned with the faithful.

There is, therefore, no need for us to be anxious or apprehensive about those who have departed this life before the coming of Christ.[3] But Theodore utters a word of warning to those who are scornful or sceptical about the Parousia. Although they think themselves to be safe and free to do what they will, the Judge will suddenly come upon them, so that it will not be possible for them to escape punishment.[4]

The state of the wicked may be generally described as perdition.[5] That, as Theodore asserts, is the

---
[1] 1 Thess. iv. 16.   [2] Heb. xi. 39, 40.
[3] Cp. Eph. i. 11. Those who have hoped in Christ at any time will obtain the reward of future glory. As far as is known, Theodore does not refer to our Lord preaching to the spirits in prison.
[4] 1 Thess. v. 3.
[5] Eph. ii. 5. Perdition is contrasted with salvation. Cp. John xvii. 12. The son of perdition is used of Judas Iscariot and of the man of sin (2 Thess. ii. 3).

usual term employed in Scripture for God's punishment of sinners in the future life. The degrees of punishment will be proportioned to their offences. If those who have not obeyed the gospel of Christ will be punished, then those who have slandered and persecuted believers will suffer far heavier penalties. The magnitude of the punishment of the wicked is shown by the power of the Judge, while the quality of their torments is indicated by the fact that they belong not to time but to eternity.[1]

Speaking generally, we may say that Theodore accepts the teaching of the New Testament on eternal punishment. But he is not fully satisfied with the traditional view, and subjects it to criticism on certain points. In particular, he cites the instance of those who lived in sin and ungodliness from the days of Adam till the first coming of Christ. Our Lord would not bestow on them a great reward by the resurrection, if He delivered them over to torments without end or abatement. How would the resurrection be reckoned as a boon, if unremitting punishment were inflicted on those who rise again? Who is so mad as to think that it is a great blessing for them to become the objects of endless torment? It would be more profitable for them not to rise at all than to undergo the experience of such extreme and exquisite misery after the resurrection by suffering eternal punishment.[2]

Theodore would appear then to prefer the annihilation of the wicked to their eternal damnation. However, he does not willingly indulge in these

[1] 2 Thess. i. 9.   [2] *Orig. Sin*, bk. iii, fr. 2.

LAST THINGS AND FUTURE LIFE 63

gloomy speculations, but he faintly trusts the larger hope. With him, as with Clement of Alexandria and Origen, there was a tendency to universalism.[1] This belief is founded partly on the signs of God's providence, and partly on His plan of salvation. It is evident that He wishes all men to be saved, because He cares for all.[2] He is the God of all, not the Lord of some but not of others; so it is impossible for Him to despise some as being alien to Him. Theodore would seem to protest against the doctrine of Augustine, that salvation is limited to those who have been predestinated by God's will. Our election must be ascribed to the mercy and love of God.[3] But our salvation depends to some extent on our free-will and co-operation with the Divine purpose.[4]

Just as God's providence is extended to all men, so the redemption of mankind by Christ is intended to be universal in its effect. He gave Himself for all; He was not content to undergo death for some, but wishing to confer a benefit on all in general, He took upon Himself suffering at the appointed time.[5] Our Lord, as mediator, was man, and because He shared our common nature, He was able to bestow the gift of salvation upon all. Theodore is inclined to stress overmuch the manhood of our Lord in His office of mediator, but, no doubt, this exaggerated emphasis may be corrected by

[1] Clem. Alex. *Strom.* vi. chap. 6; Origen, *contra Cels.* viii. 72. Souls will be gradually purified and evil will be destroyed. Cp. *de Principiis*, i. 6.
[2] 1 Tim. ii. 4. [3] Eph. i. 4, 5, 2 Tim. i. 9.
[4] Gal. v. 8, Phil. ii. 13. [5] 1 Tim. ii. 6.

other parts of his teaching. The main point for him is that Christ came near to all men by His own nature, and that, by suffering, He conferred a benefit on all men.

In accordance with the Divine scheme of salvation, Theodore believed in the final restoration or renewal of the whole creation.[1] As we have noticed already in considering Theodore's anthropology and soteriology, the whole universe, including man, was intended by God to be a harmonious unity. God had made the whole universe as one body, composed of many members, both intelligible or rational and sensible or material orders. He moulded one living being, man, to claim his affinity with the invisible natures by his soul, and to be joined by his body to the visible natures. Man was therefore, as it were, the friendly link of the whole creation, as all things were united in him. But death was brought in by our sin; the bond between the visible and invisible elements was dissolved.[2] The soul was separated from the body, which underwent complete dissolution, and this brought the dissolution of the unity of the whole creation.

God, therefore, restored or renewed all things in heaven and earth through Christ. He made His body incorruptible and impassible by the resurrection, and reunited it to His immortal soul, so that it could no longer be separated and suffer corruption. In this way He has, it seems, forged a friendly link for the whole creation. This is called the consum-

[1] Eph. i. 10, *cp*. Photius, *bibl. Cod.* 177.
[2] *Cp*. Rom. viii. 19.

LAST THINGS AND FUTURE LIFE 65

mation of all things, because all things are collected into one whole, and look to one point, in mutual harmony. This was the original intention of the Creator, who planned His whole scheme from the beginning for that purpose, which He has now fulfilled with great ease in those events which appear to have happened in the life of Christ. However, this consummation will be in the future life, when all men and the intelligible powers should look to Him, and keep enduring peace and concord with one another. It will be the complete fulfilment of Christ's prayer for unity between God the Father, Himself, and all men, and the hope of St. Paul will be perfectly realized that God may be all in all.

The main outlines of Theodore's doctrine of God and man have now been described, and it remains to consider them in relation to modern science and psychology. But before we turn to that side of the subject, it may be convenient to refer briefly to modern opinions of Theodore's orthodoxy. Though adverse opinions have been expressed about him in modern times, we find that those scholars who are most competent to judge his doctrine are reluctant to condemn him. Dr. Swete, a most careful and impartial scholar and a profound student of Theodore's works, expressed the opinion that he was entirely unconscious of deviating from the doctrine of the Catholic Church and that, so far from being a wilful heretic, he was led astray by his vigorous opposition to Apollinarianism and other errors.[1] Professor Tixeront speaks rather more severely on

[1] Swete, vol. i, Introduction, lxxxvi.

the subject. " He (Theodore) employs many inaccurate expressions, and defends certain propositions that are heterodox, at least in their obvious meaning. . . . He assuredly deserved condemnation, if only for the false interpretations to which his writings easily lent themselves."[1] But, if a theologian is to be blamed for the false interpretation which others put upon his doctrine, then very few scholars of ancient or modern times would escape condemnation. The most favourable estimate of Theodore's theology is given in a recent work, entitled *Christianity in History*.[2] It is stated there that " Theodore of Mopsuestia, one of the most modern minds of the Ancient Church in psychological insight as well as in historical methods of exegesis, came nearest to a true solution." We agree, in the main, with this estimate, and shall endeavour to prove in the ensuing chapters that Theodore's doctrine is most easily reconcilable with modern science and psychology. We do not claim that either of these departments of knowledge is infallible, but they are bound to exercise some influence on the theology of the future.

[1] Tixeront, *Histoire des Dogmes*, vol. iii, p. 21.
[2] *Christianity in History*, Bartlet and Carlyle, p. 279.

CHAPTER VI

THEODORE'S RELATION TO MODERN THOUGHT

IT is sometimes objected, even by thoughtful scholars, that the theological controversies of past centuries can have no interest or importance for men and women of the present day. Such an attitude of mind, if it were generally adopted, would be a sign of intellectual inertia, not of spiritual progress. It is a short-sighted, not a broad-minded policy to reject the theories and speculations of former ages and thinkers as sterile and obsolete. It may be frankly confessed that the general view of man's physical and mental constitution has been profoundly affected by the scientific doctrine of evolution and the analytic methods of psychology, but the problem of man's relation to God remains the same in its essential characteristics. Unless our conception of the nature of God or man is to be fundamentally altered, it is unreasonable to ignore the experience of the past, in order to concentrate our minds on the discoveries of the future. At any rate, we should be modest enough to expect that the problems which have taxed the acutest intellects of past centuries, will not admit of a short or easy solution. It may be necessary to adopt the methods of previous inquirers, and to work them out with greater thoroughness and consistency. Although we do not consider that any one method of argument is exhaustive or infallible, we admit our preference for the scientific method of induction, as applied to theology, because it leads us to argue from facts to theories, from phenomena to noumena, from man to God.[1]

The two questions about which science comes in contact and even in conflict with traditional theology, are those of the origin of man and heredity. On these two subjects scientists have established a strong claim to a patient hearing, and a ready, if not uncritical assent, because they have thoroughly investigated physical phenomena, and have collected evidence from geology, biology, and many other branches of natural science. Nearly all scientists presuppose, and the majority of theologians have accepted, the truth of the evolutionary theory as applied to the different species or genera of the animal world, including man. Even if the evidence for the theory of evolution were not so strong as it is, the scientists would be inclined to regard the alternative doctrine of the special creation of separate species as improbable, and almost incredible. On the other hand, if it were suggested that they must choose between evolution by mechanical means and creation by the Divine will, the theologians would declare that this is a false antithesis. Evolution is not a creative force of itself, but is simply the method by which God

[1] Gore, *Dissertations*, ii. p. 205. " Theology . . . may be said to be as really inductive as physical science."

RELATION TO MODERN THOUGHT 69

has brought living things into existence. There is no need to interpose spiritual influxes to fill up the gaps in the chain of causation, because, from a religious standpoint, God directs the whole process from beginning to end.[1] Organic evolution may be defined as " a continuous natural process of racial change, by successive steps in a definite direction,"[2] but neither the process nor the direction is, as the religious thinker believes, mechanically caused and controlled.

There are two general principles on which our discussion of the origin of man from the evolutionary standpoint ought to be based. (1) Man has ascended (or descended) from lower and less highly organized forms of life.[3] (2) The evolution of the race or species has been recapitulated in the development of the individual.[4]

Differences of opinion may, however, arise as to the particular application of these general principles. If it is agreed that man has ascended from lower forms of life, how far back is his origin to be traced? It is obvious that we cannot confine ourselves to the statement that man is descended from a hairy quadruped furnished with a tail and pointed ears.[5] The nearest progenitors of man were, probably, vertebrate mammals akin to the anthropoid apes, from which various " tentative " men and the

[1] *Cp.* A. R. Wallace, *Darwinism.*
[2] J. A. Thomson, *Gospel of Evolution*, pp. 34, 39.
[3] *Cp.* Darwin, *Descent of Man*, part ii, chap. xxi, p. 385.
[4] Professor Ernst Haeckel's phrase, " Ontogenie gleicht Phylogenie," puts the case in a nutshell.
[5] *Cp.* Darwin, *op. cit.* part i, p. 206.

earliest species of the genus Homo were evolved.[1] But, as Professor J. A. Thomson has clearly pointed out, man's pedigree must be traced back from mammals to reptiles, from reptiles to fishes, and finally to the amœba or protozoon, which were the primeval ancestors of the animal kingdom.[2] How, and from what source these first living creatures originated must remain an unfathomable mystery. We may prefer to accept the scientific axiom, "omne vivum e vivo," rather than suppose that living creatures were made from the dust of the earth or compounded from chemical elements, but we must confess that no reliable evidence can be produced for any scientific theory of the beginnings of life on this planet.[3]

Reverent scientists, like Darwin, and broadminded theologians have agreed that there is grandeur in this comprehensive view of life. However, those who think that such a view is degrading and unworthy of man as he now exists on the earth, should be reminded of the undeniable fact that "man still bears in his bodily frame the indelible stamp of his lowly origin."[4] Apart from general similarity of structure between man and the higher

[1] Arthur Keith, *Antiquity of Man*, 1924, and J. A. Thomson, *op. cit.* pp. 128–30.

[2] J. A. Thomson, *op. cit.* pp. 52–56, *cp.* Julian Huxley, *Essays of a Biologist*, pp. 17, 18.

[3] *Ib.* pp. 50–52, *cp. ib.* pp. 251, 252. The latter is convinced that living matter has originated from non-living matter. But this is, in my opinion, a matter of conjecture, not of certainty.

[4] Darwin, *op. cit.* part ii, last lines.

RELATION TO MODERN THOUGHT 71

mammals, we can point to vestiges or survivals of disused parts of the body, such as the third eyelid, or nictitating membrane, the os coccyx, which, in the human embryo, clearly resembles the rudiments of a tail, and the vermiform appendix. These, and other atrophied parts, which survive sporadically in certain cases, show that the individual man, like the animals, climbs up his own genealogical tree. It is no more difficult or repulsive to believe that the human race has ascended from protozoa than it is degrading to know that the individual has developed from the fusion of a spermatozoon and an egg-cell. The point which really concerns us in human evolution is not what man has been, or is now, but what he is capable of becoming.[1] Man has travelled far in his journey towards the heights, but even now he may not have finished half his course. Progress is not automatic or inevitable; there are many cases of arrested development and degeneration in man as well as in animals, but on the whole there is a tendency towards a higher level of life.

When this account of the biological origin of man is combined with the geological estimate of the antiquity of man as dating from the end of the Post-tertiary or Pleistocene period, i.e. 20,000 to 30,000 years ago, the inquiry into the possible existence of a first man or first pair of human beings seems to be futile and superfluous. Whether the historic races

[1] *Cp*. Browning's *Paracelsus*:
"All tended to mankind
And, man produced, all has its end thus far:
But in completed man begins anew
A tendency to God."

of mankind were developed from a single human pair, or a pair of anthropoid ancestors,[1] is a matter of comparative indifference. Whenever and wherever the first men and women appeared on the earth, they must have been entirely different, both in physique and moral character, from the Adam and Eve of Biblical tradition.

So far we have dealt only with the physical constitution of primitive man. But by applying the same methods, we can trace the development of mental capacities and moral character in primitive man. Here, again, we believe that the comparison of primitive man with the new-born infant is both legitimate and instructive. There must have been from the first some rudimentary form of mind or consciousness, and from this starting-point there was a gradual advance from reflex action and instinctive behaviour to intelligence and reason. At first man, like other animals, may have possessed the power of perceiving concrete things, but afterwards he probably acquired the capacity of conceiving abstract ideas. Even then, there is no sufficient reason for believing that all men rose simultaneously to that intellectual level in prehistoric times any more than at the present day. The African negro and the Australian bushman stand at a very low level of intelligence, but they are capable of higher development if they receive the necessary mental training.

The moral condition of primitive man must originally have been not righteousness or virtue, but

[1] *Cp.* Darwin, *op. cit.* vol. i, chap. vii, pp. 231–3, and Driver, *Commentary on Genesis*, Introduction, p. xxxvi.

RELATION TO MODERN THOUGHT 73

innocence or ignorance of good and evil. This fact has been very clearly expressed by the philosopher Hegel, who might be said to have applied the theory of evolution to the whole of the spiritual universe. " The state of innocence is that state in which there is nothing good and nothing evil for man : it is the condition of animals, of unconsciousness, where man does not know either good or evil." [1] The fall of man took place when he advanced from this state of innocence to a knowledge of good and evil. This was certainly a rise in consciousness, but there were no doubt many falls or relapses in conduct, whenever man misused his knowledge or freedom of action. Of course, a rise in moral consciousness is not to be confused with an advance in material civilization, which often entails most immoral consequences.[2]

Secondly, the fall of man may have been a process, not a single act.[3] This view agrees better with the theory of evolution, and is inherently more reasonable, because it is difficult to conceive how one sinful act, whatever it may have been, would have plunged the whole human race in total depravity. The change from unconscious innocence to conscious wrongdoing must have been gradual, not catastrophic. Lastly, the fall of man may symbolize, in a moral parable, the conflict of man's higher knowledge and will with the lower instincts and

[1] Hegel, *Philosophy of Religion*, i, p. 275 ff. (quoted by Dr. Tennant, *The Origin of Sin*, p. 196).

[2] *Cp.* Bicknell, *Theological Introduction to the Thirty-nine Articles*, p. 238.

[3] Bicknell, *op. cit*, p. 240.

impulses, which he has in common with the animals.[1] These instincts and impulses are neither good nor evil in themselves, but neutral. They are the raw material of moral character, but the finished product, whether it be virtue or vice, is due to the operation of the will. In the same way, the will, rightly or wrongly used, may be the source of holiness or sin. These natural powers and faculties, with which man has been endowed, can, however, become sinful, if they are used contrary to the welfare of our fellow-men or to the known will of God.

The progressive development or the retrogressive degeneration [2] of the individual or the race is closely connected with the scientific problem of heredity. The subject is fraught with difficulties, and needs careful and unbiassed investigation. Unfortunately, confident assertions are more frequently found than cogent demonstration.[3] We need to review the facts, so far as they can be known, and examine the evidence before we can draw any definite conclusions.

It is convenient to begin with an accurate defini-

[1] *Cp.* Archdeacon Wilson's address to the Church Congress of 1896 (Dr. Tennant, *op. cit.* p. 82). "Man fell, according to science, when he first became conscious of the conflict of freedom and conscience."

[2] The degeneration of a family or a nation cannot be denied; but total depravity is not generally achieved in a few generations, as is suggested by the well-known lines of Horace:

"Ætas parentum, pejor avis, tulit
nos nequiores, mox daturos
progeniem vitiosiorem." (*Odes*, bk. iii. 6.)

[3] Such plays as Ibsen's *Ghosts* and the novels of Zola are founded rather on romantic imagination than on scientific research.

RELATION TO MODERN THOUGHT 75

tion of the terms which are commonly used in this connexion.

Heredity is "the organic or genetic relation between successive generations."[1] On the one hand it implies resemblance between parents and offspring, because like tends to beget like : but on the other hand it does not exclude variation, because the offspring is never identical in all respects with its parents.[2] Resemblance and variation are not two separate and contradictory facts, but two complementary aspects of a single process.[3]

Heredity is a wider and more general term than inheritance. Inheritance means "all that the organism is or has to start with in virtue of its hereditary relation to parents and ancestors."[4] It may be further distinguished by its quality or its source. Inheritance is either physical, or mental and moral : it is either parental or social. The latter source of inheritance combines all that can be derived from the social environment, such as education, experience, and tradition.[5]

The physical basis of inheritance is the germ-cell,[6] and the hereditary factors or genes are carried by the spermatozoon and the ovum or their chromo-

[1] J. A. Thomson, *Heredity*, p. 13.
[2] E. Ray Lankester, *Kingdom of Man* (1907), p. 10.
[3] J. A. Thomson, *op. cit.* p. 66 n.
[4] *Ib.* p. 13.
[5] Julian Huxley, *op. cit.* p. 78. He distinguishes two forms of inheritance, the biological and experience-inheritance, by means of tradition.
[6] J. A. Thomson, *op. cit.* p. 26. Haeckel said, "We may regard the nucleus of the cell as the principal organ of inheritance" (*Generelle Morphologie* [1866], vol. i, p. 288).

76   THEODORE OF MOPSUESTIA

somes.[1] The germ-cells are continuous with the fertilized ovum from which the parental body arose:[2] on the other hand, they may show variations, which are transmitted to subsequent generations.[3] So far there is general agreement among scientists, but there is considerable difference of opinion as to the transmission of acquired characters. An acquired character is " a structural change in the body of a multicellular organism (*e.g.* animal or man), induced during the individual lifetime by a change in environment or in function (use or disuse)."[4] Lamarck formulated and illustrated the theory of acquired characters, or bodily modifications.[5] Since his time there has been a wide divergence of views on this subject. On the one hand, Herbert Spencer declared that either there has been inheritance of acquired characters or there has been no evolution: Haeckel also maintained it as a scientific axiom.[6] On the other hand, Galton doubted whether acquired modifications are really inherited, and Weismann denied all transmission.[7] Where the experts disagree, the amateur may be well advised to suspend his judgment. It is obvious that injuries inflicted or operations performed upon either parent will not produce a

[1] J. A. Thomson, *Gospel of Evolution*, p. 117; *cp.* Julian Huxley, *op. cit.* p. 137.

[2] J. A. Thomson, *Heredity*, p. 197.

[3] *Ib.* p. 192.   [4] *Ib.* p. 173.

[5] *Ib.* p. 170. The most popular examples are those of the giraffe and webfooted birds, whose bodily forms are supposed to be due to their habits.

[6] *Ib.* p. 195.   [7] *Ib.* p. 168.

RELATION TO MODERN THOUGHT 77

similar effect upon the offspring,[1] and it is doubtful whether alcoholism or tuberculosis contracted by the parents can be inherited by the children, though they probably create a physical or mental predisposition to some kind of disease.[2] The most that can safely be said is that the germ-cells may be affected by the body-cells of the parents, and will be developed in the bodily organism of the infant, but that there is not sufficient evidence for the transmission of a particular acquired character or bodily modification.[3] Without denying the importance of physical inheritance, we should attach equal importance to the social heritage which the child receives in the nurture and training of the earliest years of its life.

This question of the inheritance of acquired bodily characters bears a distinct relation to the further question of the inheritance of mental qualities and moral character. There seems to be little doubt that these are developed or acquired within the lifetime of individual persons. It is assumed by many scientists and psychologists that mental and moral qualities are transmitted in the same way and degree as the physical.[4] But if the transmission of acquired bodily characters is so doubtful

[1] *E.g.* circumcision or the removal of the vermiform appendix.
[2] J. A. Thomson, *op. cit.* p. 220, *cp.* p. 303.
[3] *Ib.* pp. 192, 198.
[4] *V.* Professor K. Pearson's "Huxley Lecture" (*cp.* J. A. Thomson, *op. cit.* p. 525), Bateson, *Genetics*, p. 34, Galton, "Programme of the Eugenics Education Society," McDougall, Sociological Paper III. I owe these references to a paper read before the Victoria Institute by Professor Caldecott on "Heredity and Eugenics."

and uncertain, a slight degree of scepticism is justifiable as to the transmission of mental or moral qualities. In what way is the process to be conceived? We agree, in the main, with Professor Ladd that " to speak of parents transmitting their minds to their offspring, in part or in whole, is to use words that have no assignable meaning." [1] Such transmission of minds, in whole or in part, would require some theory of " mind-stuff," as propounded by Professor Clifford.[2] But this is impossible, unless we hold a purely materialistic view of mind. Nor is it easier to suppose that the parental consciousness is mediated through the brain to the unconscious germ-cells. Professor Tyndall has said that " the passage from the physics of the brain to the corresponding facts of consciousness is unthinkable." [3] Even if we believe that brain and consciousness are closely interdependent, it would be necessary to explain how the brain-cells of the parents have affected the germ-cells from which the new organism is developed.

At the most, the germ-cells or the human embryo can only possess a rudimentary form of unconscious or subconscious life, and it is difficult to see how this unconscious life is related to the minds of the parents.[4]

[1] Professor Ladd, *Philosophy of Mind*, p. 361 ff. (*v.* Dr. Tennant, *op. cit.* pp. 32, 33).

[2] Professor Clifford, *Lectures and Essays* (2nd edn.), p. 284.

[3] Professor Tyndall, " Address to the British Association," 1868.

[4] There are, perhaps, some cases in which the thoughts or feelings of the mother have affected the bodily form of the unborn infant (*cp.* J. A. Thomson, *op. cit.* p. 163).

RELATION TO MODERN THOUGHT 79

Again, moral character is the product of individual actions and habits, and, as such, cannot be inherited.[1] But the instincts, which are the raw material or initiatives of character, can be transmitted through the medium of the physical organism. They seem to resemble physical impulses [2] rather than mental dispositions, and perhaps are best defined as innate and elementary tendencies to action which are common to all members of the human species.[3] Three kinds are generally discriminated, the self, sex, and herd or social instincts.[4] They may themselves go back to the " primary unconscious "[5] of pre-natal life, and, at any rate, they are the initiatives of conscious will, emotion, and intelligence. We do not inherit our parents' personal characters, which have been acquired in the course of their lifetime, but the instincts, which are the raw material of our own characters. It must be remembered that the development of character largely depends, at least in the early stages of a child's life, on parental influence and social environment. No one would deny the power for good or evil which is exercised by these two factors, but, at the same time, we must not confuse parental influence with physical inherit-

[1] J. A. Thomson, *op. cit.* p. 247.
[2] *Cp.* Dr. Tennant, *op. cit.* p. 98, where he discriminates between instinct and impulse.
[3] *Cp.* McDougall, *Introduction to Social Psychology*, p. 22, and Tansley, *The New Psychology*, p. 34.
[4] *Cp.* T. W. Pym, *Psychology and the Christian Life*, p. 16, and Tansley, *op. cit.* p. 53.
[5] J. A. Thomson, *Gospel of Evolution*, p. 90.

ance,[1] or minimize the importance of individual action.

The instincts, as we have already said, are neither good nor evil in themselves, but neutral. They may be perverted by indulgence or suppressed by asceticism, but they should be controlled by reason, and gradually sublimated for higher purposes. The instinct of self is needed for self-development, but may degenerate into self-indulgence: the sex-instinct may be purified by love or defiled by lust: the social instinct should manifest itself in comradeship, but may be degraded to hooliganism.

If, then, moral characters are not, properly speaking, inherited, and the instincts are the common roots of virtue or vice, it cannot be maintained that the children of good parents must be good, or vice versa. This hypothesis is contradicted by the facts of life and the records of history. The Emperor Marcus Aurelius had a worthless son, Commodus: but the vices of the profligate Louis XV did not descend to his grandson the pious Louis XVI.[2] On the one hand, the severity of the father may produce a reaction in the son: on the other hand, the misdeeds of the parents may serve as a warning to the children.

[1] The poet Goethe confuses the two in the following lines:
"Vom Vater hab' ich die Statur
Des Lebens ernstes Führen
Vom Mütterchen die Frohnatur
Und Lust zu fabuliren."
(J. A. Thomson, *Heredity*, p. 113.)
Only the first characteristic could be ascribed to physical inheritance.

[2] Of course, it must not be forgotten that the inheritance is dual or multiple, and derived from both parents.

The old proverb, "The fathers have eaten sour grapes, and the children's teeth are set on edge," [1] leads to the probable conclusion that the children have been in the vineyard too. At the same time it is clearly and convincingly argued by the prophet Ezekiel that the son may refuse to follow his father's bad example. The individuality of moral character and responsibility must be asserted, in spite of parental influence and social environment. The problem does not admit of a short or simple solution, but it has been neatly summed up in the shrewd and sensible words of the English divine, Thomas Fuller. After noticing in our Lord's genealogy that some bad fathers had bad or good sons, and some good fathers had good or bad sons, he remarks, " I see, Lord, from hence, that my father's piety cannot be entailed : that is bad news for me. But I see also, that actual impiety is not always hereditary ; that is good news for my son." [2] No doubt, it would be unwise to generalize from a few instances, but, at least, it may be inferred that there is no iron law of invariable transmission of moral character.[3]

Let us now consider Theodore's attitude towards the problems of man's origin and nature in the light of modern knowledge. Unfortunately, Theodore, like the rest of the Antiochene expositors, was

[1] Ezek. xviii. 2.

[2] Thomas Fuller, *Scripture Observations*, No. viii (J. A. Thomson, *op. cit.* p. 106).

[3] Euripides, like many others, was wrong in saying :
"The offspring of good men themselves are good ;
Those of the base are like their fathers, base."
(Caldecott, *Heredity and Eugenics*, p. 14.)

precluded from a scientific view of the origin of man by his insistence on the literal interpretation of Genesis. He attacks Origen for interpreting Paradise in a spiritual sense. Still, we should agree with him when he puts forward a plea for consistency. If Paradise is not to be taken literally, there is no logical reason why the creation of Adam and Eve or the description of the Fall should be accepted as historical facts. Theodore's objection that St. Paul took literally the temptation of Eve by the serpent, only shows that the substance of the Apostle's teaching must be accepted, but not the details. It must be frankly admitted that the Christian doctrine of sin and salvation cannot remain dependent on the literal belief in an historical Adam or a geographical Garden of Eden.[1]

However, Theodore's view of the origin of sin accords better with modern science and philosophy. Even according to the literal interpretation of Genesis, it could not be proved that actual sin or guilt was transmitted to the descendants of Adam. Abel was righteous, and Cain was wicked. It would be unjust for God to punish Abel for the sins of his parents, while they escaped punishment for hundreds of years. It would also be absurd to suppose that Noah, Abraham, Moses, and David were punished for the solitary offence of Adam. The visiting of

[1] " In reality the Garden of Eden was world-wide " (J. A. Thomson, *Gospel of Evolution*, p. 139, quoting Sir Arthur Keith's *Antiquity of Man*). If verbal inspiration is rejected, there is no more authority for locating the Garden of Eden in Mesopotamia than in Tibet. *Cp.* Dr. Tennant, *op. cit.* p. 145.

RELATION TO MODERN THOUGHT 83

the sins of the fathers upon the children can hardly be justified on the ground of Divine retribution, but it may be explained as an example of vicarious suffering or sacrifice. The prophet Ezekiel appears to have advanced beyond the morality of earlier times when he asserts the fact of individual responsibility for personal sin. "The soul that sinneth, it shall die." [1]

Again, Theodore rightly points out that the source of sin is not the nature, but the will. This is not a superfluous or meaningless distinction. The nature is the sum of our common inheritance: the will is the power of individual action. We should not, it seems, misrepresent Theodore by saying that he meant by nature what we mean by instincts. He applies this theory of human nature to the Virgin birth. The nature which was assumed by our Lord from the Virgin Mary was endowed with normal instincts, but was preserved from sin by the power of the Divine will working upon the human will.[2] We cannot argue a priori that the Virgin birth must have produced a definite moral effect, or that spiritual qualities, such as holiness, could not have been mediated by physical means. It would be better to estimate the value of the Virgin birth not so much by the absence of human fatherhood as by the presence of the Holy Spirit.

Though Theodore attacks the doctrine of original sin, he admits that human nature is originally imperfect, and that we have a powerful inclination to evil, however it was acquired. The scientific

[1] Ezek. xviii. 20.   [2] *Cp.* Dr. Tennant, *op. cit.* p. 167.

theory of heredity agrees with the theological doctrine of original sin in one point, that tendencies are inherited. But they may be good as well as evil.[1] Original sin, scientifically explained, is aboriginal instinct. The primitive man was rather an undeveloped animal than a fallen angel. In the same way, the new-born infant must be regarded as an immature, not a depraved creature. We cannot accept the words of the Psalmist about himself being conceived in sin as meaning that the process of sexual intercourse is itself sinful, nor can we interpret the words of St. Paul, " children of wrath," as referring to infants, but rather to adults who have formed bad habits and committed wrong actions. Until the will has emerged, no germ of evil or sin can be said to exist in the individual child.[2] The universality of sin must be explained, not by the universality of animal inheritance or instinct, but by the universality of will.[3] Ethics must be based on a rational and scientific psychology. We propose, therefore, to discuss the question of the origin and nature of the soul, and its relation to the body.

None of the traditional theories of the origin of the soul is free from difficulty or objection. The theory of pre-existence, as taught by Plato, and accepted by Origen, has never obtained any hold on religious or philosophic thinkers of later

---

[1] Bicknell, *op. cit.* p. 233. *Cp.* G. Frenssen, in his novel, *Hilligenlei*, chap. xviii. p. 349, " Erbsünde gibt es nicht. Erbübel gibt es, und Erbgut."

[2] Dr. Tennant, *op. cit.* p. 103.   [3] Bicknell, *op. cit.* p. 237.

RELATION TO MODERN THOUGHT 85

times.[1] Traducianism is an untenable theory of the soul, which cannot be transmitted from, or generated by the parents. Creationism, which asserts that each human soul is created from nothing by God, appears to postulate a special creation, which we have rejected for the origin of species.[2] However, there is more to be said for the modified form of Creationism, which was propounded by Aristotle and adopted by Thomas Aquinas. The latter taught that the human embryo was successively informed by the vegetative, sentient, and rational soul,[3] or, again, that souls were created together with bodies, and infused into them.[4] We should be prepared to accept this theory, if the different kinds of soul were interpreted as different degrees of consciousness. The human organism passes through various stages of growth from unconscious to conscious life, and, after birth, advances to full self-consciousness. It is difficult to determine at what point the human soul begins to exist, but at any rate there seems to be continuity of development before and after birth.[5] Most modern psychologists are agreed that the soul, or mind, or self, does not

[1] The idea finds beautiful expression in Wordsworth's " Ode on Intimations of Immortality."

[2] M. Maher, *Psychology*, pp. 572, 573.

[3] Aristotle (*de An.* ii. 3) calls them τὸ θρεπτικόν, τὸ αἰσθητικόν, and τὸ διανοητικόν. Plato divided the soul into three elements of reason, courage, and desire (*Rep.* iv. 439D, *Tim.* 70).

[4] "Fatendum est animas simul cum corporibus creari et infundi."

[5] Dr. Tennant (*op. cit.* p. 32) rightly says, "The origin of the soul is gradual, and its existence a matter of degree."

88 THEODORE OF MOPSUESTIA

The soul, or mind, can be analysed or divided into certain powers or faculties. These may be variously described as reason or cognition, feeling or affect, will or conation. A faculty has been defined as "the proximate ground of some special form of activity of which the mind is capable."[1] There is a modern prejudice against the use of the term "faculty," and a preference for some other term, such as activity. But neither term denotes any reality or operation separate from the soul or mind itself. It would be generally admitted that reason, feeling, and will are convenient abstractions for the different activities of the soul. Reason and will obviously do not exist *in vacuo*, or apart from a thinking and willing subject.

There is a more serious objection against the traditional psychology, that it gave undue prominence to the reason and ignored the lower forms of consciousness, such as the instincts and the complexes related to them.[2] Though reason is the peculiar quality of man, yet the instincts form the groundwork of the whole structure of the mind.[3] It has been already pointed out that there are different degrees or levels of consciousness. Besides the conscious or self-conscious activity of the mind, there are, no doubt, subconscious impressions, desires, and mental processes, which are generally described as due to unconscious cerebration.[4] Though from its very nature the subconscious region of the mind is somewhat obscure and indefinite,

[1] Maher, *op. cit.* p. 36.
[2] Tansley, *op. cit.* p. 21.
[3] *Ib.* pp. 34, 181.
[4] Maher, *op. cit.* pp. 355, 357.

modern psychologists attempt to distinguish between the primary unconscious and the secondary unconscious or fore-conscious.[1] The primary unconscious is the seat of the primitive instincts, and the secondary unconscious contains all the memory traces and impressions which have been made in the course of the individual life.[2] To the fore-conscious region of the mind belong also the complexes, or groups of ideas invested with emotion, partially or entirely repressed. They are either common, as related to an inherited instinct, or individual, as characteristic of a particular person.[3] This analysis seems to indicate that the different levels of consciousness are not isolated, or, so to speak, watertight compartments. There must be some definite and constant means of intercommunication. Emotions and desires are repressed into the subconscious region of the mind, while instincts and impulses rise up into the conscious life. It is a fascinating subject and likely to yield fruitful results to the investigator of normal and abnormal religious experience, but it will not be relevant to our present purpose to treat it at any length, because the ancient theologians do not seem to have considered the question of the subconscious region of the mind at all.

Theodore does not appear to have speculated on the origin of the soul, like Origen and Tertullian. In speaking of our Lord's Incarnation, it will be remembered that he insists on the fact that the Word was in the man from the very first moment of

[1] Tansley, *op. cit.* p. 53. [2] *Ib.* p. 55. [3] *Ib.* p. 61 ff.

conception.[1] It would seem, then, that the soul began to exist, at least potentially, from that moment, and in that case Theodore would be inclined to the Traducian view. He holds, indeed, that the soul is invisible and immortal: still, he does not believe in the pre-existence of the soul, but in its coexistence with the body.

Theodore agrees with most modern theologians and philosophers in his conception of human personality. Like Chrysostom and other Antiochene fathers, he was a dichotomist. It is not certain whether he derived this view from Aristotle or the New Testament. But we are convinced that neither Biblical tradition nor Greek philosophy gives any sure support to the trichotomist theory. The evidence of the later books of the Old Testament is doubtful, as *ruach* (spirit) is not always to be distinguished from *nephesh* (soul).[2] St. Paul and the writer of the Epistle to the Hebrews mention both soul and spirit,[3] but the rest of the New Testament makes no such distinction. Plato divided the soul into three elements of reason, courage, and desire,[4] of which the third was more akin to the body, but these should be regarded as different activities of the soul. Aristotle distinguished three kinds of soul, the vegetative, sentient,

[1] *De Apollin.* bk. iii, fr. 2.

[2] Con. R. H. Charles, *Eschatology, Hebrew, Jewish, and Christian*, p. 92.

[3] 1 Thess. v. 23, Heb. iv. 12. The latter may have been influenced by Philo.

[4] Plato, *Rep.* iv. 439D, *Tim.* 70.

RELATION TO MODERN THOUGHT 91

and rational souls,[1] but they should rather be described as different faculties or degrees of consciousness. Anyhow, for the majority of modern theologians and philosophers soul and spirit are synonymous terms.

Again, Theodore taught that the soul and the body are distinct entities, but they are united in one person, without any confusion. It is this connexion between body and soul which we wish to compare with modern theories. If we put aside materialistic or idealistic forms of monism, which deny the reality of one of these elements of personality, we find only two theories which attempt to explain the relations between body and soul, namely psycho-physical parallelism and psycho-physical interaction.

The former theory admits that the physical and psychical processes are equally real, but denies that there is any causal relation between them. The only relation is that of concomitance. The two processes run, like two railway trains, on parallel lines towards the same destination, but there can be no intercommunication between the two series of events.[2] This hypothesis, however, creates an unintelligible dualism in human experience, and is bound to give way sooner or later to some form of

---

[1] Aristotle, *de Anima*, ii. 3. We leave out of account the other two faculties, τὸ ὀρεκτικόν (the appetitive) and τὸ κινητικόν (locomotive). *Cp.* Raven, *Apollinarianism*, p. 191. He has shown quite clearly that both Plato and Aristotle are dichotomists. Even the Stoics give no support to the trichotomist theory. They held that the soul (ψυχή) was a breath (πνεῦμα) pervading the whole body (Adam, *Texts to illustrate Greek Philosophy*, p. 40).

[2] McDougall, *Body and Mind*, p. 131 f.

identity-hypothesis or monism. In that case, body and soul are only two aspects of the same underlying substance.[1] Herbert Spencer, for instance, says that "mind and nervous action are subjective and objective faces of the same thing."[2] But the concomitance of two facts, which even Spencer admits to be different, does not prove identity. The case of self-consciousness is not parallel, because the subject and object are assumed to be the same.

The other theory of psycho-physical interaction does not labour under the same difficulties. It may not solve all the problems of human personality, but, in our judgment, it agrees best with the facts of human experience. This theory, simply stated, declares that there is reciprocal action and reciprocal dependence of our bodily and our psychical processes.[3] Body and soul react upon each other: the experience of daily life demonstrates the effect of the body upon the mind, and vice versa. The feeling of pain does as a rule excite the emotions of sorrow or anger: the emotion of shame, aroused by some unworthy or disgraceful action, is outwardly expressed by blushing or shrinking from the society of other men. Of course, there are many reflex or instinctive actions which do not appear to correspond to any definite mental process. We do not profess to understand fully the complex machinery of the human body or the mysterious operations of the human mind. It is difficult and perhaps undesirable

---

[1] Maher, *op. cit.* p. 505.
[2] Spencer, *Principles of Psychology*, p. 140.
[3] McDougall, *op. cit.* p. 230 f.

RELATION TO MODERN THOUGHT

to draw a sharp and rigid distinction between the bodily and mental activities of a human being, but it is our firm conviction that theologians and philosophers of ancient and modern times are working on the right lines when they affirm at the same time the distinction of body and soul, and their reciprocal action or dependence. Though Theodore distinguishes the two natures of body and soul, yet he affirms their mutual co-operation, and, on this account, his doctrine appears to approximate to the theory of psycho-physical interaction.[1] It remains to be seen how this psychological theory can be applied to the relation of the two natures or wills in the person of Christ, and the relation of God to man.

[1] Cp. *de Apollin.* bk. iv, fr. 3 and *de Incarn.* bk. xiv, fr. 3.

CHAPTER VII

THE RESULTANT DOCTRINE

THE doctrine of man, as a being consisting of two distinct but interdependent elements, body and soul, must, first of all, be applied to the Incarnation. The statements of the Chalcedonian definition and the Athanasian Creed are almost too familiar to need repetition. Our Lord is declared to be perfect God and perfect man, consisting of flesh and a reasonable soul. This doctrine may seem to be so clear as not to need any further explanation. But if we are to elucidate any further the terms of this definition, we must follow the example of the Antiochenes, including Theodore, and take our starting-point from the manhood of Christ.

Our Lord, as we all confess, was perfect man. But the term "man" may be used at least in three different senses. Man may be used in the abstract sense, as denoting human nature or mankind. It is agreed that our Lord was man in the sense of possessing a human body and soul. But some theologians wish to go further, and assert that our Lord had an inclusive or universal humanity.[1]

[1] Moberly, *Atonement and Personality*, p. 86. However, Bishop Temple (*Christus Veritas*), p. 218, says that "there is no 'general' humanity, in which the Divine Word could be

THE RESULTANT DOCTRINE 95

This statement seems hardly credible if it implies that Christ included in Himself all men, past and future, good and bad. It would be better to say that Christ was the ideal or representative man, because He expressed perfectly the idea of man which existed in the mind of God at the beginning, but which was realized perfectly at the Incarnation.

Thirdly, man may denote an individual. We should rightly refuse to call our Lord a man or an individual,[1] if it were inferred that He was just one member of a class or one unit of a series. On the other hand, the idea of an impersonal manhood is equally open to objection. It suggests a sort of vague abstraction, which was appropriated by the Divine being, while the Gospels give us a clear picture of a real and unique individuality. The truth appears to be that our Lord had no separate or independent personality as man, and that can be secured in other ways than by the hypothesis of an impersonal manhood.[2] Similarly, we should demur to the ascription of an eternal humanity to God. It is no doubt true to say that the idea of man

clothed, apart from particular centres of experience, but the Divine Word took to Himself human experience in one such centre, so completely subsuming the human personality that God and Man in Jesus Christ are one Person." (*Cp.* p. 150.)

[1] Mackintosh, *Person of Jesus Christ*, pp. 385, 388.

[2] Strong, *Manual of Theology* (2nd edn.), p. 130. Gore, *Belief in Christ*, pp. 224, 227–8. *Cp.* R. Seeberg, *Grundwahrheiten der christlichen Religion* (1910), pp. 115, 116. " Jesus war ein Mensch, kein leeres Abstraktum Menschheit sondern ein individueller reicher Mensch mit einem mächtigen persönlichen Leben." That, I believe, was Theodore's own view (*v.* p. 44).

existed in the Divine Mind from all eternity, but, unless we are to eliminate entirely the conceptions of time and space, man did not really exist till the Creation, nor did our Lord really exist as man till the Incarnation.[1]

Further, we believe that our Lord, as man, was perfect in nature and character. Yet we feel bound to claim that perfection is not a static condition, but a dynamic process. No doubt our Lord was perfect at every stage of His human development, as boy, child, and man. Yet we must attribute a real meaning to the phrases in St. Luke's Gospel, and the Epistle to the Hebrews, which clearly state that He grew in wisdom and was made perfect by obedience and suffering. We do not suggest for a moment that Christ progressed towards divinity, or that He was a man who, somehow or other, became God.[2] That is a piece of purely pagan mythology, which sang or fabled of demigods and deified heroes.[3] We admit that there is an affinity between man and God, because man was created in the Divine image. But affinity does not necessarily issue in identity. Man may and ought to become more like God in character, but he does not, therefore, become

[1] Apollinarius was accused of teaching that the manhood was heavenly or eternal, but he really meant that the Incarnation was the eternal purpose of God (Raven, *Apollinarianism*, p. 216 f.).

[2] *Cp*. Kidd, *History of the Christian Church*, vol. iii, p. 408. This does not represent adequately the view of Paul of Samosata, still less those of the other Antiochene fathers.

[3] *Cp*. Hor. *Odes*, iii. 3:
"Hac arte Pollux et vagus Hercules
Enisus arces attigit igneas," etc.

THE RESULTANT DOCTRINE

God.[1] God and man are two distinct orders of being, and there is no reason to suppose that one will evolve itself into the other. Again, we should repudiate the latent assumption that any man could be perfect apart from God.[2] The best of men can only come near to perfection by personal union with God. Even that degree of union is partial, and occurs at irregular intervals. But our Lord was perfect man, because from the very first moment of His human existence He was completely and inseparably united with perfect God.

When we consider the Divine aspect of the Incarnation, it is necessary to be very exact in our definition of the doctrine. We believe that Christ was truly God-in-man. Now God, by becoming incarnate, must limit Himself, or express Himself within the limits of human nature.[3] The first mode of operation must imply that He divests Himself of some of His metaphysical qualities, such as omniscience and omnipresence. These powers cannot be fully exercised within human limits. The Gospels bear witness to some limitation of our Lord's power and knowledge, however we are to explain these facts.[4] But, is it not possible, instead of a Kenosis of the Godhead, to postulate a

---

[1] R. Seeberg (*op. cit.* p. 116) quotes the phrase of pious believers that we must become " gleichsam Christusse " (as it were Christs). But this is the mystical language of old-fashioned pietism or new-fangled theosophy.

[2] *Cp.* Weston, *The One Christ* (1907), p. 127. " Perfect humanity is God-aided humanity. Perfect manhood is manhood indwelt by God." *Cp.* p. 291.

[3] Weston, *op. cit.* p. 144.   [4] Mackintosh, *op. cit.* p. 469.

98 THEODORE OF MOPSUESTIA

"Plerosis" of the Manhood?[1] God dwelt in Christ as fully as He could dwell in a human body and soul, and manifested to the highest possible degree the moral qualities of holiness and love. These are the qualities which appeal most to the hearts and consciences of men, while a display of superhuman knowledge or power might confound without convincing them. We are not denying that our Lord's miracles were signs of Divine power, but they were even more signs of Divine love.

We may also endeavour to throw more light on the doctrine of the Incarnation by examining the conception of the Word. We agree with those scholars who trace this idea to its origin in the Targûmim rather than in Philo. The Memrā expresses most nearly the Jewish idea of Divine revelation. It represents God in His Divine activity. So St. John describes the Word as the agent in creation, as well as the perfect self-expression of God in the Incarnation. The conception of St. John has been summed up by a modern scholar in these words: "The Logos, now manifest in Jesus, is but a name for the one God, as He ever goes forth to the world in self-revealing act."[2]

The same conception may be found in the writings

---

[1] Mackintosh, *op. cit.* p. 494.

[2] *Ib.* p. 435. It is interesting to compare the words of a modern philosopher, Professor Unamuno (*Tragic Sense of Life*, p. 164). "Not because He thinks can God be God, but because He works, because He creates; He is not a contemplative but an active God." Goethe represents Faust as interpreting the opening words of St. John's Gospel in this sense. "Im Anfang war die *That*" (*Faust*, part i).

THE RESULTANT DOCTRINE 99

of the great fathers of the church of Alexandria. Clement of Alexandria and Athanasius regarded the Divine Word as the expression of the Divine will. Clement was trying to prove to the heathen that the Christians believed in one First Cause or Principle, and that Christ was the living manifestation of the Supreme Being in this world.[1] So he said, " This is Christ, this is the Word of God, the Will of the Father " ; or, again, " The Word of the Father . . . is the all-potent Will."[2] Athanasius had to perform what was in some respects a more difficult task. He was arguing with the Arians, who alleged that the Eternal Word had been begotten by the Father's will. He refuted them by pointing out that the Word was an eternal distinction within the Divine Being. " He himself is the living Counsel of the Father, by which all these things were made. How can the Word, which is the Counsel and Will of the Father, be made by will and volition ? "[3] These expressions, taken by themselves, may appear to be abstract, and inadequate to bring out the truth that the Word is really personal. But they can be translated into a concrete form, if we say that the Word is " God in action."[4]

Again, there is a growing if not a prevalent tendency to interpret the mode of union between God and man from the Antiochene standpoint, *i.e.* to

[1] Clem. Alex. *Strom.* bk. v, chap. xii, bk. vii, chap. i.
[2] *Ib.* bk. v, chap. i, and *Exhortation to the Heathen*, chap. xii.
[3] Athan. *Or. contra Arianos*, bk. iii. 63, 64.
[4] Gore, *Belief in Christ*, p. 122.

express the fact of the Incarnation in terms not of substance but of will.[1] It is true that the categories of nature and substance are enshrined in our creeds and definitions, and we cannot entirely dispense with them. Nature is a somewhat abstract, but still a convenient term to denote the sum of the qualities of a concrete person, God or man : substance, at least in its original sense, denotes the real being who is the subject of these qualities.

There is no need to set will in opposition to nature or substance, either by drawing a rigid distinction between will and nature or by exalting will above substance. Will is one of the constituents of Divine or human nature ; it is the main activity of a conscious being. Will, it may be said, is simply the self in action.[2]

If these facts are borne in mind, we may attempt to express the mode of union between God and man in Christ in terms of consciousness and will. Even so, we are faced with the same difficulty of distinguishing between God and man, and yet maintaining a real union in one Incarnate Person. It is not sufficient to say that Christ was God and man : we must affirm that He was God-in-man.[3]

Let us apply this argument first to the Divine and human consciousnesses of our Lord. It is impossible to represent Christ as possessing two consciousnesses

[1] Temple, *Foundations*, pp. 226, 247.

[2] *Ib.* p. 247. Mackintosh, *op. cit.* p. 417. " The ultimate and central reality of things is Will."

[3] Moberly, *Atonement and Personality*, p. 97. " By looking for the Divine side by side with the human, instead of discerning the Divine within the human, we miss the significance of them both."

THE RESULTANT DOCTRINE 101

placed side by side, and operating independently of each other.[1] The human consciousness was certainly developed later than the Divine consciousness : but the Divine consciousness was mediated through the human consciousness. However much we admire Dr. Sanday's bold and original theory of the subliminal consciousness being the seat of the Godhead, we feel bound to reject this hypothesis.[2] At best, the theory could only be applied to the period of pre-natal or infant life. If a truly human development is to be ascribed to our Lord, it may be granted that the consciousness of an infant is not equal in degree or extent to the consciousness of a full-grown man. Yet God was in the human organism from the first moment of its existence. Personal unity can only be achieved by maintaining that our Lord became more and more fully conscious of Himself as God-in-man.[3] The exact moment at which our Lord fully realized His divine Sonship cannot be fixed, but it must be put back to the earliest years of His earthly life.

Just as self-consciousness is a vital experience of Divine and human personality, so the central and dominant faculty or activity of every personal being is will. It is not our intention to advance the rival claims of reason or will,[4] because personality,

[1] Gore, *Belief in Christ*, p. 227. Cp. *Dissertations* (1896) II, p. 97.
[2] Sanday, *Christologies, Ancient and Modern*, p. 159 f. See criticism in Mackintosh, *op. cit.* pp. 487–90.
[3] Weston, *op. cit.* pp. 152, 159.
[4] One thinks of the scholastic controversy between the Thomists and the Scotists.

rightly considered, is a unitary and indivisible whole: but the contention is surely valid that God or man is as much an active as a rational being.[1] Therefore no doctrine of the Incarnation can be completely satisfactory unless it attempts, within the limits of our human intelligence, to solve the problem of the relation between the Divine and human wills in the Person of our Lord.

While, on the one hand, we must repudiate the view that the Divine and human wills of our Lord operate independently or even in opposition to each other,[2] we are bound to maintain the distinction between the two wills. The human will follows the Divine will, and yet is perfectly free: it is not absorbed in, or appropriated by the Divine will, so as to lose its distinct individuality. Yet it is doubtless true to say that there was only one working agent, and only one personal action of the God-man.

The question may be approached from the human or Divine side. From the former standpoint, Christ is the Man whose will is perfectly united with God's will.[3] He acted throughout His earthly life exactly as God would have Him to act. Not only was the object of His will or purpose identical with God's purpose, but the willing subject was one and

[1] *Cp.* p. 98 and John v. 17.

[2] *Cp.* Formula of the Sixth Council of Constantinople, A.D. 681 (Hahn, *Symbole*, p. 173).

[3] Temple, *Foundations*, p. 248, "He is the Man whose will is united with God's"; Mackintosh, *op. cit.* p. 417, "The will of Christ as Son is one with God's will ; . . . it is one identically"; and Dr. McNeile, *Concerning Christ*, p. 134, "One Man has made His human will identical with God's will."

THE RESULTANT DOCTRINE

the same, because He was one with God. It is quite true that two men may have the same object of will or purpose, but they still remain separate individuals, and their individual actions are not identical. A great saint may to a unique degree fulfil the will of God, but he and God do not constitute one personal being. Just as soul and body coexist in one human being, so God and man coexist in the one Person of Christ.

Again, if we regard the life of our Lord from the Divine standpoint, we should explain it by saying that the Divine will worked through the human will.[1] God was in Christ, and acted in and through Him. Yet the Divine action was not limited to the human soul of our Lord. In that way it is possible to interpret the traditional view that the Word was born in the manger at Bethlehem, and at the same time was Lord of the universe.[2] God may have expressed His will in other ways unknown to us and in other parts of the universe, but the perfect and final expression of His will for us is His self-revelation in Jesus Christ.[3]

However, some critics of theology may object that the coexistence of two wills in one Person is

---

[1] Weston, *op. cit.* p. 169.

[2] *Cp.* Cyril of Alexandria's *Ep. Synodica* (Heurtley, *de Fide et Symbolo*, p. 191), "The Word of God, while He is hypostatically united with flesh, is God and Lord of the universe," and the hymn of Thomas Aquinas, "The heavenly Word proceeding forth."

[3] Temple (*op. cit.* p. 222) quotes the lines:

"For God has other Words for other worlds,
But for this world the Word of God is Christ."

psychologically inconceivable. Though we may not be able to return a complete answer to this objection, we should like to point to the analogy of the relation between body and soul. The theory which appeared to fit best the facts of human experience was that of psycho-physical interaction. So the relations between the Divine and human wills, or between God and man, can be best explained by the hypothesis of spiritual interaction. At all stages of the religious history of mankind, God has acted upon the human soul by revelation and inspiration, and the human soul has reacted in varying degrees to the influence of the Divine Spirit. This process of Divine Immanence has culminated in the Incarnation. It may be admitted that no natural metaphors are adequate to express spiritual facts, but, at least, it seems more appropriate to draw our analogies from psychology than from physics and chemistry.[1] When we think of the union of God and man, or the interaction of the Divine and human wills, we must resolutely eliminate all ideas of spatial juxtaposition or of physical combination.[2] The interaction between God and man in the Person of Christ was of the closest, completest, and most permanent character. He never acted as God or as man independently, but always simultaneously as God-in-man.

So far, our main object has been to estimate as fairly as possible the permanent value of the Christology historically associated with the school

[1] *Cp.* Raven, *Apollinarianism*, pp. 258, 266.
[2] *Cp.* Gore, *op. cit.* p. 227.

THE RESULTANT DOCTRINE 105

of Antioch, and represented in its clearest and most consistent form by Theodore. But any theology, however intellectually satisfying, will remain to a large extent morally sterile, unless it can be brought into vital and intimate connexion with the religious life.[1] If our theory of the Incarnation is at all adequate, it must fit in with the religious experience of the normal Christian.

It is possible to express the facts of the Christian life, like the doctrine of the Incarnation, in terms of will. The analysis of the relations of God with man in religious experience has been done so thoroughly by Dr. Relton in his stimulating book, *A Study in Christology*, that it is superfluous and almost impertinent to repeat the process at any length.[2] There is only one aspect that needs to be clearly exhibited, namely the prominent part which the Divine or human will takes in religious experience. A careful study of the subject ought to show that the Divine will never coerces or absorbs the human will, but always assists and co-operates with it.

The normal modes of Divine action upon men are grace, revelation, and inspiration.

The literal meaning of grace does not throw much light upon its nature, except to show that it is a free gift of God, and not the effect of any inherent necessity or external compulsion. The definition which brings out most clearly its essential character

---

[1] *Cp.* Goethe's *Faust*:
"Grau, teurer Freund, ist alle Theorie, und grün des Lebens gold'ner Baum."

[2] Relton, *A Study in Christology*, pp. 171-95.

is "the power of God working in the soul of man."[1] The grace of God, whether it is imparted by the Father, the Son, or the Holy Spirit, is really the working of God's will upon the will of man. Sometimes the human being is almost unconscious of the Divine action, like the baptized infant or the uninstructed heathen, but nevertheless the reality of the Divine operation is not to be denied. Grace may, in certain cases, anticipate the working of the human will, but it does not annihilate its freedom. It does not coerce, but it co-operates with the human will. The action of God upon man can become fuller and more frequent, but man still retains his self-consciousness and individuality.[2]

The same conditions are observed by God in His self-revelation to mankind. The content of His revelation is largely determined by the capacity of man to receive it. The idea of progressive revelation solves the difficulties which have arisen from the different conceptions of God's nature and purpose, which have prevailed at various stages of history. "God . . . speaks daily in a new language by the tongues of men; the thoughts and habits of each fresh generation and each new-coined spirit throw another light upon the universe, and contain another commentary on the printed Bibles."[3] The word of God, in the fullest sense, is a clear and consistent declaration of His will. His purpose, which is our salvation and final perfection, does not change,[4]

[1] Relton, *op. cit.* p. 181. *Cp.* Bicknell, *op. cit.* p. 243. Grace = God Himself at work in us. *Essays, Catholic and Critical*, p. 227.   [2] Phil. ii. 13.
[3] R. L. Stevenson, *Lay Morals*.   [4] 1 Tim. ii. 4.

THE RESULTANT DOCTRINE

but its fulfilment is advanced or retarded by our understanding of or obedience to His will.

Again, because we believe that God treats men as free and rational beings, we can no longer accept the theory of verbal or mechanical inspiration. We have ceased to hold that the writers of the Old or New Testament were the amanuenses of the Holy Spirit, or that the prophets and apostles were the passive recipients of the Divine afflatus. There is, no doubt, an apparent loss in this change of view. It is difficult to determine how far their utterances are affected by the period or environment in which they lived. They can no longer be regarded as infallible, and yet they were assured of the Divine guidance in their search for the truth.[1] Even that knowledge depends upon a man's earnest endeavour to do God's will.[2]

The human response to the Divine action takes the form of faith or conversion.

No attempt can be made here to adumbrate the psychology of faith. Suffice it to say that faith, as defined somewhere by Dr. Swete, is a "moral act of the will."[3] The intellect may test and weigh various arguments which are advanced for believing this or that theological doctrine, but, when they have been fairly and fully considered, they must be accepted or rejected by the will. Belief in a person's statements or credentials involves an intellectual process, but trust arises from an exercise of the will, and manifests itself in action.

---

[1] John xvi. 13.   [2] *Ib.* vii. 17.
[3] *Cp.* Inge, *Faith and its Psychology*, chap. ix.

Conversion, as a religious experience, has attracted a great deal of attention from modern psychologists.[1] Here, again, it is only possible to give the barest outline of their methods and conclusions. It is undeniable that conversion is in some cases a predominantly intellectual process. A pious Hindu, like the Sadhu Sundar Singh, becomes a Christian,[2] or a Protestant becomes a Roman Catholic. A change from one religious system to another must necessarily involve a mental conflict. But it is not easy to separate the intellectual and moral elements. In fact, there are more cases in which conversion is manifested by a change of heart. The hardened sinner becomes a penitent Christian or even a saint. Conversion can then be explained as a re-direction or new orientation of the will. This effect has been described in the clearest terms by one of the greatest converts, St. Augustine. " This Thy whole gift was, not to will what I willed, and to will what Thou willedst."[3] The human will is turned away from self and sin, and turned towards holiness and God.

There are two regular activities of the devout soul which tend to a union of the human will with the Divine will, namely prayer and communion.[4] The

[1] W. James, *Varieties of Religious Experience*, lect. ix. Starbuck, *The Psychology of Religion*. Thouless, *Introduction to the Psychology of Religion*, chap. xiii.

[2] *The Sadhu* (Streeter and Appasamy), pp. 5–7.

[3] Augustine, *Confessions*, bk. ix (see Thouless, *op. cit.*, p. 200).

[4] We have deliberately excluded mysticism from our consideration, because it is an abnormal condition of certain highly gifted persons, and because the soul or will is more or less passive when it undergoes this experience.

THE RESULTANT DOCTRINE

essence of prayer is the intending of mind and will towards God. It would be useless to try to deal with all the aspects and forms of prayer within the limits of a single chapter.[1] The aspect which we desire specially to emphasize is that of bringing the human will into line with the Divine will. Such an attitude towards God appears to be characteristic of the prayers of our Lord, so far as they are recorded in the Gospels.[2] Of course, our prayers are hampered by our ignorance of God's will and our frequent unwillingness to perform it. But these difficulties need not deter or dishearten us, if we are sincere and persevering in our efforts to get in touch with God. Any two human persons who desire to become or remain friends should meet to speak to one another at regular intervals.[3] So our imperfect knowledge of the spiritual world and of the Divine purpose should not prevent us from trying to bring our wills into harmony with God's will.

Whatever may be the immediate object of our prayers, the final goal of the religious life is communion with God. That has been truly defined by St. John as fellowship with God the Father and His Son Jesus Christ. The basis of such fellowship must be a real and progressive union of thought and will. The various types of human fellowship

---

[1] *Cp.* Gustav Heiler's monumental work, *Das Gebet* (München, 1923), in which the subject is discussed in all its relations.

[2] Weston, *op. cit.* p. 251.

[3] *Cp.* Heiler, *Das Gebet*, p. 491. Prayer is " ein lebendiger *Verkehr* des Frommen mit dem persönlich gedachten und als gegenwärtig erlebten Gott, ein Verkehr, der die Formen der menschlichen Gesellschaftsbeziehungen wiederspiegelt."

exhibit only a partial correspondence with this purely spiritual intercourse, because they are often dependent on external circumstances and social environment. But Divine fellowship transcends all these human limitations. God has not only manifested a perfect ideal of fellowship in His own Divine being, but He has provided for the means of obtaining and renewing that fellowship in the Sacraments of the Church. This is the union for which Christ prayed, that " they all may be one : as Thou, Father, art in me, and I in Thee, that they also may be one in us." There is no suppression or annihilation of human personality, but a sublimation and intensive realization of all the higher powers of mankind. When men attain perfect fellowship with God, they find their true joy and happiness in doing their Father's will.

The essence and purpose of the Incarnation, as we have tried to expound them, have been finely expressed by Tennyson in his preface to " In Memoriam " :

> Thou seemest human and divine,
>   The highest, holiest Manhood thou :
>   Our wills are ours, we know not how ;
>   Our wills are ours, to make them Thine.

There is only one criticism which we should like to make on this verse, namely that the study of the Gospels and of Christian doctrine leaves us firmly convinced that our Lord was a Divine-human Person, not in appearance, but in reality. He was truly God incarnate, and will remain perfect man,

THE RESULTANT DOCTRINE

possessing a glorified body and an immortal soul, and all qualities belonging to the perfection of human nature, to the end of time. That will be the sure pledge of the reality of the Incarnation, and the assurance of our transformation into the likeness [1] of One who was not only our Brother and Friend, but also our Lord and Saviour Jesus Christ.

[1] *Cp.* Phil. iii. 21, 1 John ii. 3.

INDEX

A

Adam, J., 91 n.
Adoptianism, 31
Ambrose, 52
Apollinarianism, 31
Apollinarius, 27, 35 n., 39 n., 96 n.
Aquinas, 85, 103 n.
Aristotle, 20 n., 85 n.
Athanasius, 30 n., 99
Augustine, 52, 108

B

Bartlet, 66 n.
Bateson, 77 n.
Bethune-Baker, 18 n., 46 n.
Bicknell, 19 n., 73 n., 84 n., 106 n.
Browning, 71 n., 86 n.

C

Caldecott, 77 n., 81 n.
Carlyle, A. J., 66 n.
Charisius, 11
Charles, 90 n.
Christianity in History, 66 n.
Chrysostom, 2, 3, 8, 21, 33, 35, 36, 52, 55, 90
Clement of Alexandria, 17, 63, 99
Clifford, 78
Commodus, 80
Constantine, 52
Constantinople, 2nd Council, 5 ; 6th Council, 102
Cosmas Indicopleustes, 11 n.
Creationism, 85
Cyril of Alexandria, 4, 5, 45, 46, 103 n.

D

Darwin, 69 n., 70, 72 n.
Diodore, 2, 7, 27, 33, 36
Diogenes Laertius, 29 n.
Domnus, 36, 45 n.
Driver, S. R., 72 n.

E

Ecthesis, 11 *et passim*.
Ephesus, Council of (431), 11
Euripides, 81 n.
Eustathius, 27, 34, 36
Ezekiel, 81

F

Facundus, 3, 8, 11
Flavian, 2, 3, 34
Frenssen, 84 n.
Fuller, 81

G

Galton, 76, 77 n.
Gennadius, 10
Goethe, 80 n., 87 n., 98 n., 105 n.
Gore, 17 n., 44 n., 95 n., 99 n., 101 n., 104 n.
Gregory Nazianzen, 35 n., 39 n.
Gregory of Nyssa, 35 n., 39 n.

H

Haeckel, 69 n., 75 n., 76 n.
Hahn, 46 n., 102 n.
Hegel, 73 n.
Heiler, 109 n.
Horace, 96 n.
Huxley, J., 70 n., 75 n., 76 n.

INDEX

I

Ibas, 5
Inge, 107 n.

J

James, W., 86 n., 108 n.
Jerome, 52
John of Antioch, 5
Judicatum (548), 6
Julian of Eclanum, 4, 21
Justinian, 6

K

Keith, 70, 82 n.
Kidd, 5 n., 20 n., 40 n., 96 n.

L

Ladd, 78 n.
Lamarck, 76
Lankester, Ray, 75 n.
Leontius of Byzantium, 5, 7
Lightfoot, 10
Louis (XV and XVI), 80

M

McDougall, 19 n., 77 n., 79 n., 91 n., 92 n.
Mackintosh, 44 n., 95 n., 97 n., 98 n., 100 n., 101 n., 102 n.
McNeile, 102 n.
Maher, 85 n., 86 n., 87 n., 88 n., 92 n.
Manichæism, 11
Marius Mercator, 5, 11
Moberly, 94 n., 100 n.
Monothelitism, 46

N

Nestorius, 11, 46

O

Origen, 32, 33, 63, 82, 84, 89

P

Pæanius, 1
Paul, St., 9, 10, 14, 16, 20, 42, 44, 47 n., 51, 55, 82, 90, and notes *passim*.
Paul of Samosata, 20, 27, 29, 34, 41
Pearson, 77 n.
Pelagius, 21
Peripatetics, 29
Philo, 90 n.
Photius, 8, 11, 52 n.
Plato, 20 n., 84, 90 n., 91 n.
Polychronius, 1
Pringle-Pattison, 87
Pym, 79 n.

R

Rabbulas, 5
Raven, 35 n., 38 n., 91 n., 96 n., 104 n.
Relton, 105 n., 106 n.

S

Sanday, 101
Seeberg, 95 n., 97 n.
Simon Magus, 53
Sorley, 22 n., 87 n.
Spencer, 76, 92 n.
Stevenson, 106 n.
Stoics, 91 n.
Strong, 95 n.
Sundar Singh, Sadhu, 108
Swete, 4 n., 7 n., 65, 107, and notes *passim*.

T

Tansley, 19 n., 79 n., 86 n., 88 n., 89 n.
Temple, W., 94 n., 100 n., 102 n., 103 n.
Tennant, 73 n., 74 n., 78 n., 82 n., 84 n., 85 n.
Tennyson, 86 n., 110
Tertullian, 18, 52 n., 89
Theodora, 6

INDEX

Theodore of Mopsuestia, *life*: birth, 1; friend of Chrysostom, 2, 3; converted and baptized, 2; attachment to Hermione, 2; ordained priest, 2; consecrated to see of Mopsuestia, 3; death, 4; condemnation, 5; *works*: on Psalms, 7; Pauline Epistles, 8; 15 Books on the Incarnation, 10; on Apollinarius, 11; on Original Sin, 11; Ecthesis, 11; "Persian Magic," 11; *doctrine*, 13–66; modern opinions of his orthodoxy, 65, 66; relation to modern thought, 67–93
Theodoret, 5, 26 n.
Theodosius I, 3
Theophilus of Antioch, 15 n., 17, 19
Theotokos, 30

Thomson, J. A., 69 n., 70, 75 n., 76 n., 77 n., 78 n., 79 n., 82 n.
Thouless, 108 n.
Three Chapters, 5
Tixeront, 54 n., 65, 66 n.
Traducianism, 18, 85
Trinity, 24, 25
Tyndall, 78

W

Wallace, A. R., 69 n.
Weismann, 76
Weston, 97 n., 101 n., 103 n., 109 n.
Wilson, 74 n.
Wordsworth, 85 n.
Wundt, 86 n.

Z

Zoroastrianism, 11

www.ingramcontent.com/pod-product-compliance
Lightning Source LLC
Chambersburg PA
CBHW070516100426
42743CB00010B/1838